IGNITING LEADERSHIP

Ministry Principles and Priorities Leading Towards Missional Church and Revival Harvest

Contributing Authors:
Andrew Baguley, Anthony Clowes,
Ashley Cooper, Miguel Escobar,
Andy Frost, Rob Frost, Wes Griffin,
Linda Holt, Graham Horsley, Isaac Lim,
Steve Lindridge, Scott McDermott,
William Porter, Steve Wild

Foreword by:
Martyn D Atkins

Compiled by:
William Porter

MOORLEY'S Print & Publishing

ISBN 0 86071 595 7

British Library Cataloguing in Publication Data.
A catalogue record for this book is available from the British Library.

The book is set from electronic data supplied by the Authors

MOORLEY'S Print & Publishing
23 Park Rd., Ilkeston, Derbys DE7 5DA
Tel/Fax: (0115) 932 0643

Contents

Section Four – ENABLING EVANGELISTIC COMMUNITIES

Conclusion

Foreword

by Rev Dr Martyn D Atkins

Principal, Cliff College

Experts in congregational studies often suggest that the birth story of any congregation or denomination is of vital importance. The birth story of a Church, they assert, makes clear its 'DNA', its inherent nature, throughout the whole of its life. When a Church tries to depart from its very nature it goes astray; when it lives out what it is created to be, under God, it flourishes.

The articles contained here, written by Methodists, make clear some of the crucial elements of Methodist DNA. They remind us that the nature of Methodism is rooted in personal, authentic prayer and devotion. They challenge us to remember that the 'warmed heart experience', and the transformation it brings about, is at the core of our tradition. They recall that Methodism was raised up to spread 'scriptural holiness' – a complex doctrine to define but certainly one involving spiritual disciplines, a heart for the lost and a commitment to engage society with the challenge of the gospel and the inherent justice of God's kingdom in a number of ways. They lay out for us the essentially evangelistic nature of Methodism, born out of a deep love of Christ, a sincere confidence in the gospel and a complete reliance on the prevenient work of the Holy Spirit in both the believer and the 'world'. They declare, almost instinctively, the grace of God: Father, Son and Spirit. In short they make clear what is best and precious about our vital nature as Methodists.

The result is challenging, inspirational and compelling. This book will evoke in some readers a renewed confidence in evangelical Methodism as one of God's great gifts to the whole Church. It will awaken in some readers the sense of listening to beautiful music, almost forgotten, not heard for a long time, but strangely familiar and very welcome.

Whilst I was a theological student, a good number of years ago, I had a poster on my wall. It pictured a cartoon caterpillar climbing a twig and the caption read 'please be patient, God isn't finished with me yet!'

This is true not only for individuals but also for congregations and cells. God's renewing and re-igniting is not limited to persons but includes communities and even nations.

The articles collected together here not only remind us of the DNA of Methodism, themes deeply rooted in our birth and continuing identity. They also suggest that God is not yet finished with the people called Methodist, either individually or corporately, and, while daunting this is also incredibly encouraging.

The assertion that God is not finished with Methodism is easily accepted in various parts of the world where those in the Wesleyan tradition experience great renewal and growth. Some contributors belong to such churches and remind and challenge us that while renewal belongs to God, prayer, discipleship and evangelistic mission are never misplaced.

That God is not finished with the people called Methodist is particularly good news to those of us who live in situations of increasing secularism and severe church decline. To heed the calls here, to prayer, mission, gospel leadership and deepening personal discipleship is not, of course, to guarantee revival or growth. But it is a guarantee of the promise of Jesus that he will be with his people always, to the end of the earth.

So read on. Be inspired, be challenged, be open, be filled, and be ready to be changed, as you encounter the DNA of the Methodist movement again, and realize afresh that God is not through with us yet, but calls us on....

Martyn Atkins

General Introduction
Rev William Porter

William Porter is a Methodist minister based in Stoke on Trent, North Staffordshire. Together with his wife Karen they have helped establish Ignite Revival Network, with a heart to renew and resource leaders and the wider church towards revival and harvest.

This book has come out of an awareness of three things: pressures, windows of opportunity and a spiritual nudge.

Firstly, **pressures**. As a church leader in first a traditional rural setting and then in an urban context, 'spinning plates' has often been my common past time. The pressures of maintenance ministry can be all consuming. It takes most leaders all the time they have to keep the show going – worship services led, rites of passage conducted, pastoral care provided, administration and meetings sorted, crisis management offered – often whilst leading a number of churches. To find fresh energy for developing the mission shaped expressions of church needed to stem decline, not to mention time for strategic thinking and planning, is a tall order.

Secondly, **windows of opportunity**. If the projections are right, and 1,000 of our British churches could well close in the next decade, then church leaders have a very narrow window of opportunity in which to lead God's people in turning the tide. Without getting into the vigorous debate about church versus kingdom, and admitting that some of those thousand may need to die if new life is allowed to grow in its place, today's church situation provides a time of critical challenge for leadership. The level to which we can re-empower our congregations to find a more vibrant faith, help re-conceive church in fresh and more flexible terms than our current models, create the spiritual energy and momentum that can turn institutional Christianity into a new movement of Christian faith – all in these next ten to fifteen years - then to that level we have offered great leadership in our time.

Thirdly, **a spiritual nudge**. In the summer of 2003 for about a week (very unusually, I might add) I had a series of what I can only describe as visions whilst praying into the early hours of the morning. They were all pictures that I understood to be a call to prepare for revival and growth – images of unprepared harvest workers, ill-equipped army battalions, and unskilled fishermen. These and other visions challenged me to believe that the church has to change its attitude and mentality towards evangelism and mission, specifically to one of expectancy and urgency. Our mentality as leaders almost expects decline in church, and yet we are dealing every day with unchurched individuals who are hungry for spiritual answers. In this strange tension, where our ways of being church work less and less for more and more people, we can think afresh. We really can. We need to encourage each other to pursue what we see the Father doing, to move God's people to expect a spiritual harvest from the communities around them and then form church around what emerges as people respond to the gospel.

I hope that this book will have some obvious value during its shelf life. It is designed primarily as a resource for church leaders. The themes encourage you to develop key priority areas that could revolutionise the effectiveness of your ministry and ready your churches for more Spirit-inspired mission. The themes are not a group of add-ons to an already overwhelming 'to-do' list of ministry tasks. Rather they are foundational pillars in building God's house, core priorities that should underpin all the activities that you do. Neither are they limited to just you as the leader. It is important that you personally absorb these ministry priorities. However the real key to fruitfulness here is to change the culture of your congregation; to splice these into their spiritual DNA. When you have helped your lay people to absorb these priorities then change really is on the way.

'Igniting Leadership' is not a programme driven manual. It is however an encouragement that, in building these priorities into your congregational ministry and mission, you ready yourself more for the moving of God's Spirit in and through you. You set yourself in a good place for God to use you in these coming days.

This book is also valuable because of its authorship. It is a mix of contributions by fifteen church leaders from across the globe. They are all, in some way, involved in cutting edge church mission and growth. They are all open to the Spirit. It has a unique potential as an anthology by group of Methodist leaders working for the renewal of the church in the UK and around the world. This series of reflections are valuable in understanding what pillars or principles of ministry should best strengthen churches and move them more towards being effective in Spirit-inspired mission.

Acknowledgements

I want to express my thanks for those who have helped the vision for this book to come to reality. Thanks especially to the contributing authors: Isaac Lim, Wes Griffin, Scott McDermott, Miguel Escobar, Rob Frost, Graham Horsley, Steve Wild, Linda Holt, Andrew Baguley, Andy Frost, Steve Lindridge, Ashley Cooper and Anthony Clowes. They have fitted in a writing project into the middle of busy diaries in a gracious way, and have engaged with the issues of this book wonderfully. Thanks, too, for those who have helped proof-reading: Lainy, Karen, Paul, Tracy, Ashley, Moira, Andrew, Joan, Nick, Linda, Stuart, Leny & Gordon. I'm grateful to John and Peter at Moorley's Print & Publishing for their advice, help and hard work in pulling this project off. Thanks to Phil Nankivell for his excellent, eye-catching artwork and cover design. A particular word of acknowledgement goes to artist Tom Hammond, and to Carol Littleton Shay and the Littleton Studio for permission to include Tom's print "Revival in Progress".

This book has come out of a vision for missional church and revival harvest that has been held by the Ignite Revival Network core team and was spurred on by the Singapore 2004 1st International Prayer Conference for Wesleyans in Renewal. It reflects the burden on the hearts of my wife and I for the church of the future, and I hope resounds with the hearts of many in church leadership. I thank Karen and our children Joshua and Sarah for their patient support in my putting this book together.

This book is dedicated to the memory of my grandfathers, Luther and Wilfred, who faithfully carried the flame of the gospel in their generation, and longed that we would continue to do so in ours too.

William Porter – November 2005

Preface

Ready for harvest

'In the middle of a still, humid summer's day, the farm workers are idling time away. Ripe corn fields are all around them, but they are resting in the sun, chatting, some snoozing. They are passive, oblivious to the urgency of attending to the over-ripe harvest. Others tinker with rusty farming machinery nearby, which stand quiet, obviously not used for a long time. Harvesting equipment is inadequate and unprepared. Suddenly, from the corner of the fields, massive combine harvesters, manned by eager workers, power into action, moving in purposeful sequence together, to gather in the ripe golden corn. The farm hands, caught off guard, stumble to their feet and rush to their ageing machines. As engines struggle into life, the labourers, with a surprising fresh sense of purpose, line up with others to join in the harvesting of the great crops before them.'

This was one of the prophetic pictures the Lord showed me a year ago about the state of our church. We are marked by a variety of attitudes to the decline we face and the situation in our nation. Some have their heads in the sand, unable to face the reality of the moment; others are using coping mechanisms to manage decline pastorally. Some brave ones are boldly rationalising and pruning to enable growth, and a few visionary ones are seeding new experimental forms of church presence. Not many are actually expecting a large harvest from their efforts. Prayer is not mobilised, missionary strategy not acted upon, members are not empowered, and leadership is not prepared for the harvest that is growing around us. If we do not wake up to the potential of this season, we will be caught off guard by others who are better positioned for harvest, spiritually and naturally. We need to quickly enable an attitude of expectation and a culture of spiritual readiness to touch people who are ripe and desperate for the love of Jesus.

Why do I say this? There are trends, unnoticed by many, that point to impending harvest. When we look at the explosive global prayer movement at the moment, the unsatiated hunger for spirituality in people all around us, the common bonding of hopes and fears in which international crises that have captured ordinary people's attention, we see a ripe harvest field. Yet if we see only the desperate state of church decline nationally and locally around us, we can lose perspective. We can feel perpetually inadequate for the task and forever by-passed by our society's fast-tracking into post-Christian post-modernity, rather than harvesters poised to capitalise on ripe fields of God-opportunity.

For example little in the life of the Argentinean church of the 1970's looked promising for the evangelistic harvest of the mid 1980's under the ministry of Carlos Annacondia. Evangelical churches were by and large small, insular, marginalised and feeling powerless. The national trauma of the Falklands War aftermath also created an openness amongst the churches for a fresh wind of the Spirit, and the space for visionary evangelists and church leaders to rise and capitalise on the moment.

The story of Jesus' hands-on teaching with the disciples in John chapter 4 vv27-38 is very pertinent for our situation today. In this episode Jesus, of course, has been about His Father's business in touching yet another life with kingdom grace. Now in the aftermath of the wonderful changed heart of the Samaritan woman, and the stirring of spiritual interest in the local village, Jesus' disciples return from a shopping trip, and they find their values and expectations colliding with His.

In a dialogue typical of many, Jesus debriefs the Twelve after yet another ministry situation they failed to capitalise on. He chides them for being preoccupied with material interests (v31), unaware of a spiritual harvest around them (v35), and passive spectators to Jesus' ministry (v32). Does that challenge us? How often do we keep our sights low, consumed by maintaining church rather than turning ourselves inside out in expressions of kingdom grace? Does our faith stretch to personal risk taking in reaching out to others, expectant that God can use even me to bring a seeker to Christ? In contrast Jesus calls them, and us, to have a heart for the Father's work (v34), spiritual sight to see the harvest fields (v35) and a renewed commitment to join in the harvesting of the kingdom (v38). He is looking for a new mentality, a new motivation and a new commitment.

Of course, what I say has to be put into context with the need for radical movement to be present in a new way within our culture, to incarnate church in the midst of the people. We need help to re-learn in what ways to live and tell the gospel so that it truly resonates and challenges the people of our communities. Yet, as Jesus knew, the battle in the lives of leaders is often the battle for our hearts – to sustain our motivation, commitment, mentality and values about ministry.

Principle-led Values

In an age of experimentation of what it is to be church, the language of techniques, conferences, models, theories are all in fashion. But so too is that of atmosphere, relationship, authenticity and encounter. Maybe it is the inevitable clash within us of the modern and the post-modern. Much can be said about the trend of image without substance, in our changing culture, and yet the yearning is for *both* image and substance, of the prophetic models *and* the deep values. The desire is for the 'called-ness' that overcomes the instinct for 'drivenness'. Desperation for success with church will lead to driven leaders and models, unless we respond to a calling of God to respond to His building of church in our generation.

As much as we need good theology we also need authentic spirituality. The key place of nurturing the soul of leaders is that of principle-led values: something to live for that lines up with our inner spiritual reality, the bedrock of our conviction.

We may be aware of the shift from personality to character ethic, from an outside-in to an inside-out approach to personal development in leadership teaching and mentoring. Stephen Covey, author of 'The Seven Habits of Highly Effective People', speaks succinctly about this:

> 'The Character Ethic is based on the fundamental idea that there are principles that govern human effectiveness - natural laws in the human dimension that are just as

> real, just as unchanging and unarguably "there" as laws such as gravity are in the physical dimension...principles are guidelines for human conduct that are proven to have enduring, permanent value.'[1]

Just as there are natural principles, so there are godly principles for living. So, for example, a godly principle endorsed in the book of Proverbs is that 'the fear of the Lord is the beginning of knowledge' (Prov 1v6). It is espoused by some biblical scholars as, in fact, a broader key to understanding the Hebrew Scriptures and to a life lived in covenant relationship with God. Inherent in godly values are both theology – what I believe – and spirituality – why it touches my heart. The 21st century brave new church requires leaders with these godly values, both conviction and substance, a fire burning through their spiritual bones. When we look at the three spheres of relationship that a Christian leader engages with – God, world, church – we can identify core principle-led values that can be fostered to harness a leader's sense of calling with the great need of the church today. They are: passion for Christ; compassion for the lost and broken; vision for churches living in revival. We will look at each briefly in turn.

Passion for Christ

In one of the most revealing of gospel exchanges with his disciples, Jesus catches up with Peter many years after his initial calling. Memories now are the heady days of excitement in laying down career to follow a dream. Taken as read is the gradual absorbing of Jesus' kingdom values and teaching. Second nature is the life of mission and miracles the disciples were now participants in. All now in tortuous dislocation because of Peter's weakness of character and with words. The denial of His Lord left Peter questioning his entire purpose. He is a leader dealing with a past, with disappointments, failure, lack of confidence. And in John Ch 21 Jesus forces the issue by asking one question.

If I had been Jesus, there are many questions that would have been on the tip of my tongue. 'Peter, do you know how much you have

---

1 Covey, Stephen, The Seven Habits of Highly Effective People: powerful lessons in personal change (London: Simon & Schuster UK Ltd, 1989) pp33 &35.

hurt me?' 'What is this flaw in your character that led to your caving in?' 'Can I ever trust you again?' Jesus knew the answers to all those questions anyway. The one thing he wanted to ask Peter was 'Do you love me?' To interpret that you might say, 'Is there a passion in your heart for me, Peter?' 'Despite all the failure, after this long journey, even looking into the chasm between what you hope for and what you are, is there a passion burning in your heart for me?'

It is a question true for us too. If the chief of the apostles is a model for us here, our leadership is only as authentic as our commitment of love is to the Lord. It is He who called us and him we follow, even in the middle of busy local church or kingdom ministries. Our passion for him is key to our fruitfulness in life and ministry. Many things might work to rob or erode us of our love for Jesus. Failure might, stress could, pleasure often will, sin certainly does.

If these things erode, then what restores this passion? Restored passion is nurtured through an awareness of the presence and fresh reality of Jesus and, through that, regaining a conviction of the gospel. Again, if this story is a narrative parable, then it is only when Peter is confronted by the risen Jesus that he is able to face his true values. Before then he was only wrestling with himself and the voices in his head. For a leader the constant awareness of Jesus' presence is the most vital check and balance in keeping us true to our calling. Many things that rob us of passion are at the root the result of a life not exposed to His transforming presence. How we build that pursuit for intimacy with God into our lives is very individual, but foundational it certainly is. As Tommy Tenney, revivalist and author of 'The God-chasers' writes:

> 'God is everywhere, but *He doesn't turn His face and His favour everywhere*. That is why He tells us to seek His face. Yes, He is present with you every time you meet with other believers in a worship service, but how long has it been since your hunger caused you to crawl up in His lap, and like a child, to reach up and take the face of God to turn it toward You? Intimacy with Him! That is what God desires.'[2]

---

2 Tenney, Tommy, The God Chasers (Shippensburg, PA: Destiny Image Publishers, 1998) p38.

God seems to have a way, through many passion-robbing experiences, of showing us again the bottom line, why we joined in the first place. The bottom line of the gospel is that 'He died for all, that those who live should no longer live for themselves but for him who died for them and was raised again' (2 Cor 5v15). This is not just an issue of leaders needing to be humbled by our weakness. It is more an issue of always realising our need of Jesus. My only reason for being in ministry of any shape or description is that He called me. My ultimate goal is to please Him not people. I owe my life to Him for He died for me. It's all for Him. That is the bottom line. It's the words of Peter when he says, 'Lord, You know all things. You know that I love you'.

That passion regained becomes the fuel for conviction about the gospel of Jesus as 'the power of God for the salvation of all who believe' (Rom 1v16). Many leaders have had the initial zeal of their call and the fire of faith once nurtured in quashed through academic theological training. This highlights, not that academic theology is bad for you, rather that it is only one side of leadership formation. As Nigel Wright, scholar and churchman writes about this issue:

> 'This is one reason why it is not enough for a theological education in the service of the church to teach people how to become critical. They also need to burn with conviction if they are to do anything other than help people embroider pre-existing, inherited beliefs. To win people to belief and faith takes the dynamic of conviction, commitment and enthusiasm.' [3]

For the elderly Paul, an apostle of lifelong discipleship by the time he wrote Philippians, he had great conviction about his gospel and a consuming love for his Lord. His ultimate value system was in reference to Christ. 'I consider everything a loss, compared to the surpassing greatness of knowing Christ Jesus my Lord, for whose sake I have lost all things' (Phil 3v8). He was truly living the acrostic of faith: *Forsaking All I Trust Him*. A passion for Jesus does not have to be robbed or eroded from our lives. It can rise to a constant flame, and positively consume us, as it did Paul. It can

3 Wright, Nigel, *Re-imagining evangelicalism* in Cray et al, *The Post-evangelical Debate* (London: SPCK, 1997) p106.

be, at times, all that has kept us going in leadership. It should be our foundational value. For the apostle John, recording Jesus' priestly prayer in John 17, remembers His petition to His Father 'that the love You have for me may be in them, and that I myself may be in them' (John 17v26). Is there any higher privilege than to share with God the Father the same passion He has for His Son as we engage with his call to follow him?

Compassion for the Lost and Broken

In the gospels, Jesus is always an inspiring role-model, illustrating the values he wants his disciples to exhibit. On one occasion, Matthew brilliantly captures his attitude to the pressures of ministry that surrounded him. It is in the middle of the summary of Jesus' preaching tours around northern Israel (Matthew 9vv35ff). In a whirlwind of teaching and healing, Jesus is continually faced by crowds of people, looking to him, needing his attention. How often leaders face exactly this. Constant pressures, demands, people intensive tasks of ministry. 'When he saw the crowds...' (v36), how would we end that phrase if it described our ministries? '...He said: "enough is enough!"; "I need a day off!" "I can't give any more!"; "I'm putting the answer machine on!"? Instead Jesus exhibited great understanding and empathy: 'he had compassion on them, because they were harassed and helpless' (v36). What an inspiring attitude, and what a challenge to my often selfish and very human response to demands on my time and energy.

It is not often the big, unique crises that cause us problems. The Asian Tsunami disaster of 2004 demonstrated an amazing display of generosity by people the world over, all caught up in a shared moment of compassion for the victims of the tragedy. It is rather the daily, never ending, job-never-finished, people demands that wear us down in ministry. 'Compassion fatigue', a condition that charities are well aware of, affects people when it is just one more appeal through the door, the straw that breaks the proverbial camel's back. In the same way leaders constantly move from one problem to another, and another. Whether extrovert or introvert, we can face this wearing down of our ability to react to people the way we know we should, with compassion.

Thankfully Jesus gives us some clues in this story as to how we can be more like him. One clue is that He 'saw' the crowds. Jesus' amazing discernment about individuals here extends to his insight into the hearts of the crowds around him. He sees what the Father is doing, and focuses his attention on what God shows him. We can assume rightly here that this sharing of the Father's heart leads to an overflow of compassion from Jesus again and again. How often do we pause within ourselves, whilst amongst the crowds, to let God show us what He sees in the lives of the people around?

Another clue is how Matthew describes what Jesus sees. The crowds were 'harassed and helpless, like sheep without a shepherd' (Matthew 9v36). This phrase 'sheep without a shepherd' is actually an insult to self-respecting Jews of Jesus' day. For one of the predominant images in the Old Testament about God's people is that they are His flock, the sheep of His pasture. The most loved Psalm 23 addresses God as the psalmist's own shepherd. Jesus here realises that the crowds have forgotten who they are and to whom they belong. Jesus identifies people's great need for God and his kingdom life, and that draws out His compassion and anointed ministry.

What do we see when we look at the people around us? Do we see problems or individuals to love in Jesus' name? Do we gauge ministry to others as kairos moments or tight slots in ever busier diaries? Our compassion comes as we come close enough to God to see crowds with His heart – the world as full of lost and broken people. We are always called to minister to the broken of our communities – the poor, marginalised, sick and needy. We are very aware of the broken lives of people surrounding us. How aware are we that we are also always called to join in Jesus' mission to seek and save the lost? An interesting shift that some evangelists are making in helping the gospel be more relevant to changing society right now is in realising that people are more lost than wrong. It is not as though the unchurched are connoisseurs of the Christian faith and have chosen moral alternatives. It is more that they are lost in a sea of spirituality and searching for what they do not know. As leaders, a major reason for our commitment to Christian ministry is ultimately that people need the Lord. We must not be apologetic about this fact. Again, Nigel Wright:

> 'Conversion is a touchstone. Christianity's astonishingly virile story from its origins in Jesus and the apostles onwards has been one of its constant ability to remake broken lives, to inspire hope and bring about personal and social transformation, and to do this in diverse culture after diverse culture.'[4]

Our compassion must flow from the heart of God to be able to sustain our action and safeguard our motivation. One great example of this truth is Heidi Baker who, with her husband, serves as a missionary in Mozambique. They head up an orphanage ministry, working with thousands of street kids who have no hope and no prospects. The demands upon them are overwhelming, yet Heidi has found a secret of keeping a Jesus perspective in the middle of great need. She relates a vision she had of Jesus that changed her perspective:

> 'I saw a vision of Jesus. I saw His face. I saw His burning eyes of love piercing through my soul. I saw His broken, bruised body. There were thousands of children surrounding Jesus. I began to weep and I cried out, "No, no there are too many!"
>
> 'The Lord replied, "Look into my eyes." My heart melted as I looked into His face. He handed me a piece of His broken, bruised body and said, "Give it to them to eat." His body became bread in my hands. I gave it to all of the children and everyone ate. Jesus said, "I died so that there would always be enough."
>
> 'After you see His face, you can never be the same. From that day forward, I have never said no to a single orphan or to an abandoned or dying child. I simply take them all. And as He promised, there has always been enough.'[5]

Compassion on the lost and broken flows from the heart of Jesus. It grows in us as a deep value in ministry whilst we engage with our

---

4 Nigel Wright, op cit, p105,

5 Baker, Heidi, in Experience the Blessing: testimonies from Toronto (Ventura, California: Renew Books, 2000) p54.

world, through Him, with all its complex problems and immense need.

Vision for Churches Living in Revival

One of the teasing dilemmas in discussions about the New Testament is that concerning Jesus' attitude to what would come after His ministry. Did he intend to start a separate church or rather establish a kingdom renewal in the heart of Judaism? As is sometimes said, 'Jesus preached the kingdom; what the disciples subsequently organised was the church'. However the bare evidence in scripture is that Jesus had a clear understanding of what He was leaving behind, as he conferred a kingdom on his followers (Lk 22v29), promised to build his church upon them (Matt 16v18), trained them in both missionary strategy (Lk 10vv1-12) and life in community (Matt 18vv15-20), and commissioning them to extend and incarnate His kingdom's rule (Matt 28v19-20).

Moreover, Jesus had a vision of the church in mind as he gave his life for the world on the cross. In Ephesians 5, the interesting passage about husbands and wives, we find an almost mystical picture of Jesus' love for the church. Within an image drawn from Jewish bridal preparation for a wedding, the author meditates on Jesus' loving preparation of the church to enable her to be his bride. For Christ 'gave himself up for her, to make her holy...and to present her to himself as a radiant church' (Eph 5v25-27). Even as Jesus died, he had a vision in mind of what his church might be. That vision of a heavenly bride is foreshadowed during the church's history particularly in times of renewal and revival, when the church is refined, cleansed, purified in ministry and refocused in mission. This is the potential of the church in our day also. Jesus has a vision of what our churches can become in the opening of the 21st century.

We know that vision is essential to a leader's capacity to lead. We lead from a future view, though anchored in the past. But for how many has the initial exciting vision and call to ministry within the church become worn down by the realities and struggles of the local congregation, so that they no longer get excited about what they were first called to?

There is a danger of becoming cynical about church, as outmoded ways of operating no longer work either for outsiders or, increasingly for regular worshippers. It is very easy to take pot shots at institutional church right now. Yet the cynic tends to become one through a loss of hope in, or inability to change, a certain situation. The antidote to cynicism about the church is a fresh vision of what she might become. The church is still God's best idea as the meeting point and focus of Christian passion and compassion. As church leader of Seeker-Friendly Willow Creek Community Church in Chicago, Bill Hybels says, 'the local church is the hope of the world'. Why? Because it is the only group of people that visibly offer the transforming love of Christ. He elaborates:

> 'There is nothing like the local church when it's working right. Its beauty is indescribable. Its power is breathtaking. Its potential is unlimited. It comforts the grieving and heals the broken in the context of community. It builds bridges to seekers and offers truth to the confused. It provides resources for those in need and opens its arms to the forgotten, the downtrodden, the disillusioned. It breaks the chains of addictions, frees the oppressed, and offers belonging to the marginalized of this world. Whatever the capacity for human suffering, the church has a greater capacity for healing and wholeness.'[6]

Our calling to lead and grow church is motivated, not out of what we so often fail to live up to, but rather the very uniqueness of church – its potential in God's hands to be a sign of His very kingdom life in our world.

There is the story of a famous sculptor who was once giving a master class. The particular sculpture he was working on was a stallion. When asked by an observer how on earth he went about chiselling out such a complex animal from a rectangular piece of stone, he replied, 'it's simple. In my mind's eye I have a clear vision of the horse within that block of stone. I then just chisel away whatever isn't horse!'

---

6 Hybels, Bill, Courageous Leadership (Grand Rapids, Michigan: Zondervan, 2002) p23.

A vision of churches living in revival isn't looking for a quick fix solution for congregations in decline. What it is calling for is a realisation that the practical strategising (both around nurturing experimental shapes of church and also shoring up declining denominations) desperately needs linking with the praying for deep renewal, and the fresh breath of the Spirit.

As both a missiologist and pastoral church leader, I have not been able to shake off a vision for revival which God has given me over the last fifteen years. Aware that language has loaded connotations, I realise that the coinage of 'revival' is a heavily used one, encompassing the history and hopes of evangelicals for hundreds of years. In some circles revival talk has never been acceptable. Even amongst sympathetic brethren, it can sometimes be seen as a pious and out dated understanding of mission - one which waits for God to bring in the converts whilst we sit within our church walls and pray. Such piety can be rightly seen as a hindrance to the brave, fresh mission thinking which engages our culture with a new vulnerability and creative authenticity.

Yet the more I read and reflect on the self-understanding of revival communities, it is precisely the reviving influence of the Spirit that each so desperately needed to enable them to be useful to God in His mission. A revival theology is, at its heart, one that looks to God to recreate a new missionary DNA in the midst of church. Forget the hagiography, ignore the excesses, and don't think in terms of 'quick fix' move of God. God is committed to His world long term. At the turn of an epoch such as we are living in, the reviving, enabling currents of the Spirit are needed over a generation or more, to turn the spiritual tide. We need Spirit-filled leaders who run in a lifetime of ministry with a vision that churches can live in revival reality – inspired afresh by the Spirit to deep repentance, attractive holiness, vibrant worship, purposeful discipleship, dynamic kingdom growth, serving and transforming their neighbourhoods with the love of Christ and enabling swathes of unchurched people to discover a living Christian faith.

Ministry Priorities

In revival times those on the cutting edge raised a banner of prayer, dug deep wells of renewal, stood tall in leadership, and ran with the gospel. Anon

Now to introduce the main part of this book. 'Igniting Leadership' pinpoints some cutting edge ministry priorities that need to be in place in His church. They are highlighted in this book for natural and spiritual reasons. I have already mentioned the ministry overload. So many people in church leadership are not sure what to concentrate on in moving congregations from maintenance to mission. To find the fresh energy and prophetic discernment as to what is the 'God thing' to do is a big challenge.

We are also living in an age of change, in which the church is becoming marginalised in influence and muted in its voice. And so we need to think prayerfully as to what God is calling us to do in terms of our cutting edge ministry as a church. In doing so God is calling us to define or, more accurately, to redefine our course as church. We cannot afford right now to merely continue the status quo for the sake of appeasing people; we need to channel our energies into the things that will make a difference in kingdom terms. We simply must be concerned with understanding God's strategy for this hour.

There does seem to be a God-breathed common purpose that is emerging, not just nationally, but internationally amongst renewal circles. These four priorities seem to be inherent in the growth of many churches inspired by God, evidenced for example, in the first International Prayer Conference for Wesleyans in Renewal – 2004 Singapore. They are themes that we can put in place in our ministry and mission. They are actually things that are there embryonically in many of our congregations, but they need to be encouraged more and more. Leaders are the catalyst behind change and have a vital role in embracing these priorities.

John Maxwell, a Christian leadership consultant and author reflects on the responsibility of leadership in creating change:

> 'Effective teaching comes only through a changed person. The more you change, the more you become an instrument of change in the lives of others'.

And again:

> 'Once the leader has personally changed and discerned the difference between novel change and needed change, then that leader must become a change agent. In this world of rapid change and discontinuities, the leader must be out in front to encourage change and growth and to show the way to bring it about'.[7]

Each section of the book covers one of four overarching themes

- mobilising a movement of prayer
- sparking spiritual renewal
- releasing radical leaders
- enabling evangelistic communities.

Within each section there are five parts – firstly a brief introduction to the theme by the editor; secondly a keynote chapter by Rev Dr Isaac Lim, which is an expansion of a series of lectures he gave at a recent IGNITE conference; thirdly an international perspective, written by a church leader from outside the UK or with wide experience outside the UK; fourthly a specific application by a British church leader; and fifthly a 'Generation X' viewpoint, in which a younger leader gives a prophetic and challenging future view perspective for the church.

The book is majoring on these four cutting edge themes of church life and ministry. It does need to be said, of course, that this is not the sum total of church ministry. I am making prior assumptions that, amongst leaders and instilled in churches, there is a clear understanding of Christian orthodoxy – the basic evangelical beliefs of repentance from sin, faith in Christ, an awareness of core gospel truths of God's creative and saving work, and a Christian discipleship that includes incorporation into the church.

It is also worth noting that we are here concentrating on cutting edge ministry priorities, not a reductionism of ministry. Our

---

7 Maxwell, John, Developing The Leader Within You (Nashville: Nelson, 1993) p73.

churches need to stay aware of the great treasures of a full-orbed church ministry and mission, one that includes long term discipleship, a multi-dimensional understanding of mission, and a connection to the life tradition of the historic church. However these four themes of engaging in prayer, renewal, releasing leaders and evangelism have often been sidelined in the life of the local church. Yet these same four are the very growth potential for churches. That is why they need highlighting as they are.

The diagram which follows gives a simple conceptual and contextual overview of the book's themes. Firstly, the key to all Christian thinking is God's great mission. All our mission ideas, hopes for the kingdom are secondary or derivative to God's mission. God is, as has been said, a fountain of sending love. Our churches' existence and mission flow from the missionary heart of God. Our mission is anchored in God's acts of salvation through the life, death and resurrection of Christ and ongoing work of the Spirit.

Secondly the overarching goal of all we are and do is participating in His extending of His kingdom rule. Our mission is future-oriented because church, society and world are being drawn into God's coming kingdom. The church is a sign of that kingdom life – not the totality, but a shadow, an approximation, a dull mirroring of it. Yet it *is* an authentic sign, one that draws people into the realm of God's love in Christ and identifies what that kingdom life might look like.

Thirdly the intermediate challenge to the church is to work towards a revival expectancy and harvest focus, as already outlined. Both fresh expressions of church and existing congregations must engage with this spiritual and visionary dimension if we are to grow significantly in the 21st century.

Fourthly, the values that leaders are called to embody, in order to be radical in our culture, are the issues of the heart that I have already discussed above – passion, compassion and vision.

Those foundations having been laid, we can now concentrate on the ministry priorities that can, God willing, lead us on a path towards a radical growth of fresh church and a harvest of people coming to Christ.

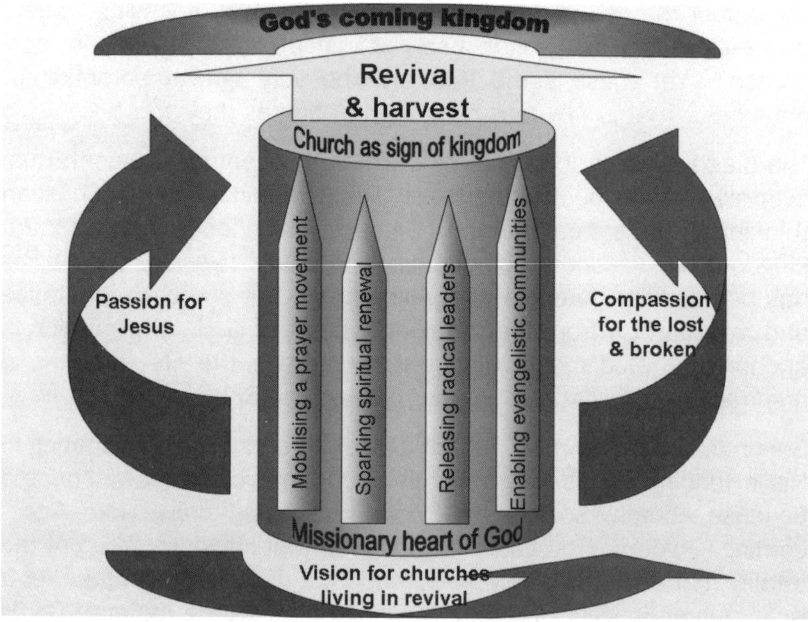
God's coming kingdom
Revival
& harvest
Church as sign of kingdom
Mobilising a prayer movement
Sparking spiritual renewal
Releasing radical leaders
Enabling evangelistic communities
Passion for
Jesus
Compassion
for the lost
& broken
Missionary heart of God
Vision for churches
living in revival

SECTION 1
MOBILISING A MOVEMENT OF PRAYER

Introduction
William Porter

There is currently an impetus in the body of Christ to go beyond sporadic prayer meetings for a few keen or pious members, towards mobilising a movement of prayer throughout the church. God is already stirring this across the world, and we are the ones who are partnering in *His* intentions.

It has been noticeable, in recent years, that there has been an ambiguous retrospective reading of the renewal of the mid 1990's by many church leaders. Some, in embracing it have been blessed and their ministries changed beyond all recognition. Others have been embarrassed or confused by it, and not known what to make of what *didn't* happen in that wave of renewal. There were undoubtedly some false hopes and misunderstandings. As a result many churches, having not understood what happened in the 1990's, have chosen to distance themselves from talk of revival, and become hardened to the dynamic of praying for spiritual awakening.

In its place there is a great deal of activism in the church at the moment – congregations trying the next idea off the shelf, the next course, programme or strategy for growth - many out of desperation. Some churches are in such panic about how to stem decline that they will try almost anything, with a consequent danger of lack of prayerful discernment.

Now the challenge, in the middle of this, is to become God-centred again. This is what the Spirit is calling us to do through a movement of prayer. In times of crisis for a nation or church (whether we are prone to activism or panic) God says to us, as in 2 Chronicles 7v14, that when the heavens are shut, when nothing is going right, when we don't know where to turn, 'If my people, who are called by my name, will humble themselves and pray, and seek my face and turn from their wicked ways, then I will hear from heaven and will forgive their sin and heal their land'. There is a divine equation of how prayer, humility and repentance can lead to renewal of life, faith and fortune.

There has never been such a tide of prayer across the worldwide church historically as there is right now. In terms of prayer rooms, prayer houses, prayer gatherings, 24/7 prayer, prayer apostles, prayer strategies for nations, what is happening is global, and it is such a God inspired happening. We can only stand in awe, and remind ourselves that, before every major move of the Spirit, there has been a prior work of prayer. The praying is the indicator of the change in spiritual atmosphere, rather like the change in atmosphere before a thunderstorm. Now if God is behind this prayer dimension, then what in the world is about to happen?

As Bob Dunnett, past vice principal of Birmingham Bible Institute, wrote on the factor of 'Extraordinary Prayer – the herald of revival':

> 'The sure and certain mark of an approaching outpouring of the Spirit has always been the emergence of this kind of prayer. No revival has come without it, and when it begins to appear on a wide front, without any obvious human prompting, we can be sure we are hearing "the sound of wind in the mulberry trees". When revival is about to break out, this kind of earnest, extraordinary prayer can pour out like a huge cataract as the Spirit floods into the hearts of God's people.'[1]

Christians of all persuasions are wondering what is coming as a result of this prayer movement; what is God doing in the middle of this? Terry Tekyl, a United Methodist Church pastor and prayer leader in USA, shared his response to this recently in an international gathering of Methodist leaders in Singapore. His strong feeling, as a result of travelling the world encouraging churches in prayer, is that the prayer momentum is leading us to become a church of God's presence – a *Presence-based church*.

1 Dunnett, Bob, Let God Arise: Making Way for Revival (London: Marshall Pickering, 1990) p119

The church could become known, not for its good programmes or its nice activities, but rather for encountering the manifest presence of Jesus in our midst by His Spirit. This is echoed by other church leaders. It is also the testimony of many people who have spent a time in a 24/7 prayer room, that they have been overwhelmed by the utter reality of God as they were praying and their spiritual lives have been deeply enriched. Prayer, worship and spiritual renewal are inextricably linked up in such a movement.

This prayer burden, stirred by God, can become the catalyst for vision. Rather than take the next good idea from the Christian conference circuit, God wants to give us His vision for how He wants to build His church in our generation, as He mobilises a tide of prayer in our midst. In Acts 13vv1-3, the church in Antioch, which was growing and dynamic, was also a church deeply in prayer. And out of their praying, God gave them a fresh strategy, a sacrificial vision, as they were led to set apart Paul and Barnabas to lead a new church planting mission amongst the Gentiles of Asia Minor.

For some parts of the church, it will be a vision for itinerant mission. Like the 18th century Moravians who, through the 1727 outpouring in Herrnhut and the establishing of the 24/7 one hundred year prayer meeting, sent out 100 evangelists across Europe and indeed the world as missionaries in the following 25 years, with an astounding clarity of the love and salvation of Jesus. For others, like the early charismatic pioneering 'Church of the Redeemer' in Houston, Texas USA, it will be a forging together in radical community living and local Spirit led mission in their neighbourhood. For others, like my own city of Stoke on Trent in the Midlands, it is a vision of one church for the city, owning the spiritual responsibility for a geographical region, with leaders and congregations drawn together in a five year journey of worship and prayer to let God impart His heart and strategy to transform a city in Christ's name.

There is a whole gamut of mission visions, one of which God might want to give to your church or ministry. But it all starts on bended knee, in God stirring our hearts to pray out of need, brokenness, humility and desperation. Have we allowed ourselves to be caught up in this prayer movement yet?

Mobilising a Prayer Movement

Rev Dr Isaac Lim

Isaac Lim is the past president of the TRAC English speaking Methodist Conference in Singapore. He now helps with the International Leadership Institute. Isaac organised the 1st International Prayer Conference for Wesleyans In Renewal in 2004. He has a global vision and has mentored many leaders.

I believe God calls us to raise Prayer movements so that we can change the texture of the church, as we seek His face.

The Vision

It is important for us, first of all, to have a vision as we mobilise a movement of prayer. What is God saying to us as a church? What is God saying about the future of the church?

When we talk about a vision, we refer to a concise picture of what we believe God wants the church to be, at some future time. We can see in our mind's eye, what we want the church to be. Without a vision, we would have no sense of direction. The prophet Habakkuk says, 'Write the vision, make it plain on tablets so that a runner may read it' (Habakkuk 2:2). In other words, your vision should be so clear that anyone reading it, can understand it and run alongside it.

When we gather for prayer, if members of our church ask us the questions, "Pastor, what is the vision of this church? Where are we heading? How are we going to get there?", what would our response be?

I remember sharing the vision that God had placed in my heart, with members of my Annual Conference in Singapore. I told them, that the vision God had placed in my heart, was for each church in our

Conference, to be an oasis of worship and spiritual renewal. The vision was to enable every person on entering the church, to experience the presence of God and depart from our church, blessed. Whether through the acts of worship, the preaching of the word, the singing of hymns and spiritual songs, the worshipper would leave the church satisfied, because he or she has met with God.

What is your vision? What is God saying to you about the Methodist church, in your country? What do you see, as the hope for the church? What is the mind of Christ concerning the church?

In 1 Corinthians 2:14-16, Paul talks about the spiritual and unspiritual person. He says “Those who are unspiritual do not receive the gifts of God’s Spirit, for they are foolishness to them, because they are spiritually discerned. Those who are spiritual, discern all things, and they are themselves subject to no one else’s scrutiny. ‘For who has the mind of the Lord so as to instruct him?’ But we have the mind of Christ” (v16).

We know in our churches, that there is present both the spiritual and the unspiritual person. Even amongst the clergy there are those who are spiritual and those who are unspiritual. The difference between the spiritual and unspiritual person, is the fact that the spiritual person knows the mind of Christ, and the unspiritual person does not (v.16).

The spiritual person not only knows the mind of Christ, he or she is also connected to Christ the Vine (John 15:5). If we are connected to Jesus, the Vine, then it invariably means that we have the mind of Christ. If we have the mind of Christ, we should then know what God is saying to us in the context of the church. If we do not know, then it is time for us to go on our knees and find out why. That is what I did.

When I was appointed pastor of Wesley Methodist Church in 1982, we had about 1200 people attending church every Sunday. I asked God what He wanted me to do. I believed God was about to bless the church further, and that it was necessary for us to enlarge the place of our tent so that we could receive God’s blessing of growth.

The first year as Senior Pastor, saw the church increase by one morning service. We originally had 4 Sunday services - 2 traditional services in the morning, 1 traditional service in the evening and one

7.30pm 'Pray and Praise' service. That same year, we added a third morning traditional service. Within a year that service was also packed with people. The Church had grown.

Knowing that further growth was forthcoming, I gathered my leaders together and shared with them my vision. I told them that God was going to further bless the church, and that it was imperative, that the church extended her facilities, to cope with the blessings that God was about to bestow on the church.

I suggested to our leaders the possibility of relocating the church to a larger site. The suggestion resulted in some reaction from the older members of the church, who felt that for sentimental reasons, the church should never be relocated. Many of them had special memories of their church – they were married there, their children were baptized there and they were not ready to relocate.

Finally it was agreed, that in order to cope with the anticipated growth, the church hall would be redecorated and serve as a second sanctuary. The church hall was subsequently redecorated, to house over 500 persons. It was in this hall that we introduced a Prayer and Praise Service, that would run concurrently with the Traditional Service in the Sanctuary.

We began the service in 1984. In one year we grew by 500 persons at the Prayer and Praise Service. The next year we introduced a second Prayer and Praise Service in the same Hall. That same year we grew by another 500 persons. In other words, in two years we grew by about 1,000 worshippers in both our Prayer and Praise Services.

We were then running 7 services each Sunday and people were pouring into the church for all our various services. By the time I left Wesley Methodist Church, at the end of 1989, we had 3500 persons attending church every Sunday. That was not all, the church would meet every Wednesday night for prayer. We interceded for the needs of our church, the work of missions and evangelism, the needs of our members; we prayed for those who were not well, for our pastors, for the various ministries as we watched God do a new work in the lives of our people at Wesley.

What is your prayer vision? What is the vision that God has placed in your heart? If you do not have a vision, you will not be able to mobilise the church to pray. The church cannot pray along with you, because they are ignorant as to where they are going.

Mobilisation Defined

Mobilisation is the ability, to rally men and women around a vision and to work towards the fulfilment of that vision. What is the vision of the church?

If you have a vision you can mobilise your people, so that they can own the vision and work towards the fulfilment of that vision. With a vision, you are better able to motivate the people you mobilise.
How do we motivate our people? Firstly, we tell them what God is saying. It took me several years before I got my Annual Conference really excited about prayer. I began with a monthly prayer meeting called the 'Methodist Prayer Network'. In this prayer network, I drew people from all the churches in our Conference for a time of prayer. I would instruct my pastors to make an announcement of the meeting in their respective churches every month and encourage them to come for prayer. We would meet once a month.

As people came, I began to tell them what God had placed in my heart, about the renewal of the church. Each time they came I would challenge them to pray for the renewal that would take place in our churches, and for God to pour His blessings and usher in a new day for the people called 'Methodists'.

Secondly, I tell them what God has promised. I share with them the enabling that comes to us, through the baptism of the Holy Spirit. I share with them the power of God at work in our lives as we trust Him. I invite them to the altar, to experience God and to receive the enabling, that comes through the Holy Spirit, and many are blessed.

After meeting for about a year, we decided to meet on a weekly basis on a Monday evening, in what was called, 'The Hour of Renewal'. At the Hour of Renewal, we would highlight one church in our Conference, for special prayer every week. We would tell the pastor of the church concerned, that we would be highlighting his church and request him to be present with his members for that particular Monday, so that we could pray for them. We would also ask him for specific prayer items, so that we could intercede intelligently, for that church. In that way, we covered every church in our Conference with prayer, throughout the year. Through prayer, we have seen all our churches being blessed by God.

Thirdly, I motivate our people by telling them that they can experience the presence and power of God when they come together in prayer. I tell them the importance of their involvement in a God-inspired vision. I tell them why prayer is important and that it is their opportunity to serve God, through the avenue of prayer. I tell them how important they are, as members of the prayer force. I then tell them the blessings they can receive, as they bless others through the ministry of prayer.

Intermittently, I will pause in prayer, and ask these prayer warriors to bring their own needs before God's throne of grace. As they have prayed for others, the church, the world, it was imperative that they prayed for themselves, and experience God in a personal way. I want them to know, that they too can experience answered prayers. I then invite them to the altar and the pastors present at the Hour of Renewal, would take time to pray for them at the altar.

I believe God wants to bring about renewal, amongst the people called 'Methodists'. This is God's moment. God is allowing us an opportunity to rise as His people. Sometimes we say to ourselves, 'We are so few. What can we do?' Do not despise small beginnings. Look at the greatness of God and cling on to what God can do.

Methodist pastors sometimes get discouraged, when they compare their church with other churches. We wonder if God has passed us by. I do not think so. I want for us to remember, that God has His timing of blessing for His people, and I believe He wants to bless us now! Are we ready to receive His blessings of renewal?

Mobilising a Movement of Prayer

How do we mobilise a movement of prayer? Begin by gathering a fellowship of like-minded believers. Sometimes that is hard work, but it gets easier as God begins to move in our midst.

In 1967, I met with a small group of Evangelical Methodists, for a time of prayer. The Methodist church then was a liberal church, and we wanted to see a change in the texture of the church, so we gathered to pray. With every passing year, we saw the evangelical base grow larger and stronger. God began to call some of us into the ministry of the Methodist Church. A few of us became pastors initially, others became active lay leaders and subsequently, more and more evangelicals joined the ministry as pastors.

Today, I would say 90% of our pastors are Evangelical Christians, 40% are charismatic pastors. The texture of the church has changed but it has taken us many years to get there. We need to begin somewhere, and we can begin by gathering a fellowship of like-minded Methodists.

Having gathered a fellowship of like-minded believers, you will then need to clarify the vision. You need to reach a consensus, as to what God is saying to the church. You need to be that spark that can bring about renewal, change and transformation. Perhaps you need to write the vision out, so that all concerned can claim ownership of that vision. You need to be of one mind.

With the vision clarified it is time to raise a prayer call with the purpose of imparting vision and gathering a larger prayer community to extend ownership. People need to own the vision and so the prayer call can accomplish that. This purpose of imparting the vision to a larger and wider Christian community, is for them to pray alongside us.

One of the things I initiated as President of the Conference was, 'The Methodist Prayer Call'. Every January 1st, members from all the churches in our Conference would gather for a day of prayer. We would meet at one of our churches and pray from 11.00am until 5.00pm. We would normally have around 400 people coming, just to intercede. We spend the day in worship and intercession, interceding for the Church, the nation, the world and those with special needs. Here, I would affirm the vision and encourage ownership.

Finally, you need to mobilise sympathetic church leaders to initiate a prayer movement, in their respective churches. When prayer becomes an important pillar in the life of every church in the Conference, the spark of renewal is lit, and the church will grow in strength to the glory of God.

The Call to Intercession
Rev Dr Scott McDermott

Scott McDermott is the senior pastor of Washington Crossing United Methodist Church, Pennsylvania, USA since 1995. He lectures in New Testament studies at Perkins Theological College, and has been involved in the Aldersgate spiritual renewal conventions in recent years. He has a big heart for prayer.

A few weeks ago a young intercessor in our church came and asked me an interesting question, "Pastor Scott, the intercessors who meet on Sunday afternoon really feel led to hold an all-night prayer meeting in our church a few Saturday nights from now. Would that be OK with you?" There was no hesitation with me. I know this man's heart, his fruit, and his passion for God. I said, "Sure, that would be great. Go for it!" And they did. All night they prayed. I joined them a few hours that Saturday evening and rejoined them again for prayer before the Sunday morning service. Even though tired, they were full of life, interceding for the advancing of the kingdom among us that Sunday morning. There is no doubt in my mind that the exuberant worship and ease of teaching and ministry that morning was aided by their relentless intercession.

God has placed a rich deposit of prayer at Washington Crossing United Methodist Church ("The Crossing"). If you look around, you see it everywhere. Our Sunday night evening of prayer continues to attract a considerable number of people for a congregation our size. People come to intercede for personal, church, national and international needs. A midweek evening of soaking prayer provides a place where people come to rest before the Lord in an atmosphere of assuring worship and quiet intercession. Numerous other ministries underscore the rich deposit of prayer at the Crossing; prophetic intercession, healing rooms, prayer advocates for our missionaries, for Israel, prayer for the nations, a prayer group for Sunday morning services, prayer emails that call intercessors to lift up strategic concerns of the ministry, to name just a few. In fact, all that we do is under-girded with prayer.

Reclaiming the Promise of Intercession

As rich as this deposit of intercession is at the Crossing, I remain convinced that God is calling us to a deeper level of intercessory prayer as a congregation. Intercessory prayer is quite simply *taking up the cause of another in prayer*. That cause may cover a wide range of concerns – healing, guidance, blessing, and any other bestowal of divine favour. In the New Testament, we frequently see this type of prayer exemplified. It seems to have been a staple of New Testament church life. Little wonder because prayer opens doors for ministry (Col 4.3), grants hope in difficult circumstances (Phil. 1.19), provides sustaining grace when we are at the end of our rope (2 Cor 1.8-11) and opens our heart to the wonders of God's love (Eph. 3.17-19). What most interests me is the way in which the apostle Paul recounts the honour, joy and privilege of intercession (Phil. 1.4; 1 Thess. 1.2). His contending in the Spirit is not burdensome, but exhilarating, filled with compassion and spiritual longing.

Yet today the thought of prayer seldom triggers the idea of privilege, joy and honour. Even in "renewal circles" it is not uncommon to hear prayer associated with "legalistic religious drudgery". It is as if the church has lost its way, its sense of wonder in intercession and with it the vibrancy and fire that once filled its prayers. At its core, it seems that the church has lost the sense of divine visitation in prayer, and without it, prayer becomes an empty and hollow shell of religious activity.

Taking a church deeper in prayer will require us to reclaim our lost heritage. One of the best descriptions of our heritage in prayer is found in Romans 8.26,27.

> 26 *In the same way, the Spirit helps us in our weakness. We do not know what we ought to pray for, but the Spirit himself intercedes for us with groans that words cannot express.* 27 *And he who searches our hearts*

> *knows the mind of the Spirit, because the Spirit intercedes for the saints in accordance with God's will.* (NIV)

I believe these verses provide three important insights about intercession.

1. Intercessory prayer comes as an invitation to pray with the Spirit. Such an invitation to join the Spirit usually begins with questions on the part of intercessors, "How am I to pray in this situation? How do I take up this cause with God?" The fact that such bewilderment even occurs underscores our weakness and with it our dependence upon the Spirit's help. These verses state that even in times when our weakness is most evident, the Spirit will join us, help us, and guide us through our prayers. This is significant in reclaiming the nature of Biblical prayer. It means prayer is not a solitary journey, predicated upon my own effort to make it work. Prayer is the work of the Spirit inviting me to join him in intercession.

   I was in a prayer meeting with my staff recently. About one-third of the way into our prayer time together, one of my staff shared a prophetic picture he was receiving. After sharing, he suggested that I pray individually for each staff member in the room. I immediately sensed the truth of his words, but felt that I needed to wait before the Lord before proceeding. That waiting granted me time to sense the Spirit's direction for those prayers. When I finally did start praying for them, the force and power of the intercession was obvious, filled with other prophetic pictures, and a deep release of anointing. One person fell off his seat onto the floor under the anointing. Another wept while others joined in strong agreement to my prayer over each person. In that moment, I was partnering with God for the destiny and calling of each one on my staff. Prayer is a partnership with the Spirit.

2. Intercessory prayer is not superficial; it often comes from the deepest part of the intercessor's heart. When we pray with the Spirit, deep longings and yearnings are often deposited into the heart of the intercessor. Verse 26 provides a description of what I am referring to when it says: *but the Spirit himself*

intercedes for us with groans that words cannot express. Without going into the multiple exegetical ways of interpreting this unusual Pauline phrase, suffice it to say, the image depicted by Paul certainly describes "impassioned longing." Whether cries in a spiritual language, or deep groans, the image of impassioned intercession cannot be dismissed.

I have participated in intercessory prayer meetings over the years, not just here at the Crossing, but elsewhere as well. Their flavour is distinct, the emotions are fervent, and its sounds are thunderous. Oh, don't get me wrong. I am not calling for a raucous and unbridled display of emotion just to create some thunder. My point is that intercessory prayer pushes us into a new frontier of spiritual experience. These deep longings represent both a deep empathy for the needs of others, and an inexpressible longing to see the victory of God expressed in some tangible form. At times these deep longing cause the intercessors to quake under the weight of their own prayers. I have seen marvellous wonders come out of such prayer meetings. Much of our present outreaches in mission around the world were birthed through just such a time of intense impassioned intercession. I can still see a group of thirty people, shaking, yelling, and crying out for God to give us his heart for the world, to open doors for us, so that we would go where he wanted us to go. Within a week of that prayer time, three doorways opened worldwide and work among the nations began.

3. Finally, intercessory prayer is about releasing the will of God on the earth. Verse 27 tells us that the Spirit intercedes according to the will of God. God's desire is to release his will through us as we join him in prayer. Prayer is never about our will, it is always about the will of God. The Lord's Prayer itself affirms that message when it says, "Your kingdom come, your will be done." This means that the invitation to prayer is essentially an invitation to join with God in doing his work in the world. John Wesley captured this idea best when he stated that God did nothing except through prayer. What a convicting thought.

Prayer then is not an option; it is rather a necessity for doing the work of God.

For me I am learning daily that the victories we long to see tomorrow are won first in prayer today. Some might ask, "Does that mean you are trying to earn tomorrow's blessing by prayer?" Nothing could be further from the truth. Prayer is not the place where blessings are earned; it is the position in which blessings are received. Prayer is the place where the work of God begins to make itself known on earth.

Taking a Church Deeper

Still one must answer the question, "How do you lead a church deeper in intercession?" Let me offer a few suggestions from what I have learned over the past 12 years in leading this ministry.

Ask God to expand and deepen your prayer ministries. The idea is this: if you want a praying church, ask God for it. While most of us recognize the need for increased intercession in our ministries, we seldom consider asking God to help us. Asking God has a number of advantages. First, it reminds us that prayer is not another program. Prayer represents our dependence upon God for all we do in ministry. A prayer-based church realises that new ministries are to be birthed through prayer and nurtured with continual intercession. What better way to begin leading a church forward in prayer than to pray. Second, when we ask God to help us, God will encourage us. In answer to prayer, God will start to stir up a fresh vision for prayer, new leadership and resources will surprisingly begin to emerge, and our eyes will be opened to fresh and innovative pathways that lead the church forward. I still consistently ask and pray for an expansion of our intercessory base here at the Crossing even with all the prayer ministry we already have. The more God gives us to do, the more we need God's help to live the divine opportunities. So if you want your church go deeper in prayer, ask God to bring that to pass.

Teach people how to pray. In other words, you lead them where you feed them. If you want your church to grow in prayer, then you must teach people how to pray. I remember when I first entered ministry over twenty years ago. The Senior Pastor I was working with told me he thought that most believers did not know how to pray. I must confess that when I heard this statement I found it unbelievable. How could Christians (people filled with the Spirit) not know how to pray? At that point, I began to study prayer seriously and I soon learned he was right. Not only did believers not know how to pray, but I discovered my own prayer life was woefully inadequate. It was a lesson I never forgot.

When I first came to the Crossing, one of the first things I did was teach people how to pray. At first I used a variety of resources to help people grow in prayer. I now use a prayer guide I have developed entitled "Fill Your Prayer with Praise". In the word "PRAISE," I highlight six basics to personal prayer. "P" stands for "praise." Our prayers begin with worship and thanksgiving to God for what he has done. "R" stands for "repentance." I must regularly allow the Spirit to search my heart, confess my sins before him and ask for forgiveness and forgive those who have sinned against me. "A" stands for "ask." In the asking stage of prayer I lift my personal requests before God and trust him for my needs. "I" stands for "intercede." When I intercede I trust God for the needs of others. "S" stands for silence. Spending time in quietness before him allows me to be still enough to know that God is still in control, and it allows me to hear his voice. And "E" represents expectation. I pray with expectation, and as I leave the place of prayer I go expecting to see answers to my prayers.

To emphasise the basics of prayer each new member of our church receives a "Fill Your Prayer with Praise" book mark, and "Ten Helpful Tips On Prayer." Of course we offer more advanced teaching on prayer as well, ranging from learning to hear the voice of God, to growing in the prophetic. At least once a year, I will underscore the importance of prayer in one of my teaching series.

Live what you teach. You cannot lead where you are not willing to walk yourself; that is also true with prayer. When I first came here, I made a commitment to become a person of intercession. I blocked out my mornings, and told the church I would not be in the office until at least 11 am throughout the week. You can imagine their response. I told them that my first requirement as a leader was to pray for this congregation and spend time in the Word. In all the years I have been here, I have made few exceptions to this commitment, and the people have honoured my commitment by encouraging me to keep praying. One of the most important things we can do as leadership is to model our commitment to prayer.

Cast the vision for prayer continually. Taking a church deeper in intercession will necessitate continually calling people to pray. I suppose by now, some of the people at the Crossing are tired of hearing me say this, but I do not apologize for it. I recognize that leadership requires communication, communication and more communication. I realize if I don't say it repeatedly, it won't be heard. I remind them of what God does through the power of prayer, the victories we have seen, and the ground that is yet to be taken. No one can sound that call like the spiritual leadership of the congregation. I find that people are hungry for leadership, spiritual leadership who would rally God's people to kingdom purposes. Just recently I stood before our congregation and gave the call again. "We must contend for new territory in prayer", I reminded them. "It is in prayer that the battles are won first." What happened! They came to pray. They know by now that what I am saying is truth.

Bless your intercessors. Intercessors are usually an interesting lot. Quite frankly I am not so sure if there is another group like them in all the church. At times they seem quite "out of the box" from your regular church members. Usually true intercessors live on the edge, pressing forward with great courage, faith, and hunger for the supernatural. They are filled with resolute commitment, uncompromising dedication, and unwavering faith. Once God gives you such a blessing, it is important for pastors to bless and encourage what he is doing among them.

One day as I was in prayer, I felt a distinct call to bless our intercessors publicly. During our next evening of prayer I called them all forward. There they stood before me, people of all ages, honoured to have me recognise them. I thanked them for the blessing they were to me, to our congregation, and I blessed them for their tireless hours of intercession. However, I did not anticipate what was about to happen. After finishing my words of affirmation over them, I proceeded to pray for them. When I did, the room seemed to erupt in deep groans, and cries. Almost everyone fell to the ground under great anointing, and the fire soon spread to the rest of the congregation that night. The results were amazing. Not only was the anointing especially strong in the prayer, but we saw some exceptional miracles follow.

Remember, allow the Spirit to guide you on the journey. This is not a scripted journey. It is a Spirit-led journey. The goal of every leader in the Spirit is to hear the voice of God, to believe, and obey. Having led this church for a number of years now, and having watched this congregation grow in prayer, I can see that God has taken us through different seasons of emphasis in our prayer ministry. For one season, I was the one who did most of the teaching on prayer in this church, both in the larger congregational setting as well as small settings. This was helpful and beneficial for the congregation because it helped to establish the priority of prayer as we transitioned to a prayer based church. Pastors often lead across key thresholds of congregational life, and in that season, that was my role. However, as the church grew, and ministries began to develop, new emerging leadership took over what I once began.

There are numerous seasons of prayer in the life of the congregation. Some of these include seasons of prayer and fasting, all night prayer meetings, 24/7 prayer events, and city wide prayer events, just to name a few. The key is to discern the season for you. When the season comes, go with it. When the season is over, learn to walk away and trust God.

A rich deposit of prayer in the life a congregation is instrumental for the work God wants us to do. When we reclaim the promise of intercession, we are beginning to step forward with the Spirit's help into the unfolding of God's plans for ministry. I have never regretted one moment I have spent in prayer with God, neither has this congregation. We live for those moments because we realize that in them God is speaking, healing, and empowering us to do the work he has called us to. Wherever you are today in your prayer life, will you ask God to take you deeper in intercession? Go ahead and go for it!

Keys to Breakthrough in Prayer

Linda Holt

Linda Holt is a partner of Interprayer, a resourcing prayer agency based in the UK, and of Deborah Arise International, a prophetic European women's network. She is also a lay leader of a growing local church in Helsby, Cheshire, and stimulates prayer wherever she travels.

Our God of the Breakthrough!

> *'The Breaker (The Messiah) will go up before them. They will break through the gate and go out through it and their King will pass on before them, the Lord at their head'. Micah 2:13 Amplified Bible.*

There are many situations in our own lives, in our churches and in our nations, where we need to see a breakthrough in prayer. One of the names in the Bible for the God we serve, is 'the Breaker'. The picture is, of One who will go through the gate before us, preparing the way. Our God is the God of the Breakthrough! Hallelujah!

We come across this name, in the story of David's battle with the Philistines, as recorded in 2 Sam 5 and 1 Chronicles 14. The Philistines had heard that David had been anointed king and this disturbed them greatly. The enemy is always disturbed by the anointing of God and will try to oppose it, in any way he can. The Philistines came and spread themselves in the valley of Rephaim or the 'valley of the Giants'. David's immediate reaction was to enquire of the Lord, as to what he should do. He was told to go and fight, and was given a promise of victory.

> *'The Lord has broken through my enemies before me like the bursting out of great waters. So he called the place Baal Perazim (Lord of the breaking through)'. 2 Sam 5:20.*

We are reminded of this victory in Isaiah 28:21, in the context of God speaking about coming judgement for His people, who had rebelled and trusted in their own sources of confidence, rather than in Him, the Living God.

God wants us to experience breakthrough, as we pray for the situations, that He has put on our hearts. What are the areas, where you need to see such a breakthrough?

Before we consider some keys to praying for breakthrough, we need to understand some of the 'giants' the enemy will try to put in our way, to stop us.

Several years ago, we decided in our family, that we were going to change our spare room and make it into a prayer room, for the use of the family. We wanted a place of safe retreat, where we could be creative in prayer, somewhere where we could pray in an undisturbed way. So, we took out as much furniture as possible, and arranged the room in a way, that would make a place of peace, that would encourage prayer and meeting with God. For a few days after doing this, the enemy unleashed a barrage of opposition, including sickness, pastoral problems in the church, electrical appliances breaking down and plumbing problems. It was chaos! All we had done was re-arrange a room, but it was our intention to seek God, and the enemy knew this!

What are the giants that the enemy will try to use as you pray for breakthrough? Disappointment and frustration are commonly used. He wants to throw you off track, and tell you, that you are wasting your time. You may see no change in the natural realm for a long while and feel that nothing is different. You will find yourself fighting distraction from other things trying to fill your time - even 'good things'. Fear may be used to try to freeze you into inaction. The 'spirit of religion' may rise up to oppose you. You may find yourself battling lethargy and tiredness. So take authority over these giants, in the name of Jesus. You need to take hold of the vision that God has given you, and pray unceasingly, until you see your breakthrough.

Keys to breakthrough in prayer

The Bible passage that we are using to draw these keys from, is the story of Joshua and the battle of Jericho. Jericho was an important city in the Jordan valley. The name Jericho may be interpreted in several ways. Some say it could mean 'the City of Palms' or 'the City of the Moon', suggesting that the inhabitants may have worshipped a moon goddess there. It was on a major trading route and therefore, a key city for commerce.

Key one – spy the land

> 'And Joshua son of Nun sent two men secretly from Shittim as scouts saying, "Go view the land, especially Jericho"' Joshua 2:1

The first key in seeking breakthrough in prayer, in a given situation is to have a clear and discerning understanding of the problem. Often, we can be tempted to pray about presenting symptoms of a problem, without digging deep enough, to discern the root cause underneath. There may be many factors contributing to a blockage. Praying superficially is rather like cutting off the branches of a bramble, whilst leaving the roots in the soil. The problem will present itself again, even as the bramble will spring back to life – often with renewed vigour! As intercessors, we need to ask the question "Why?" Why is this situation as it is and what has happened to make this situation come about? Is there an underlying spiritual problem? What exactly is going on?

At one time, we lived in a manse right by a busy main road. In our first nine months, in this house, there were nine accidents on the road right outside. The screech of brakes, the bang, broken glass, rushing out to see if we could help, became quite routine. Accidents were getting more serious, until one day just before church, we rushed out to find a van on its side. Thankfully the driver was not seriously hurt, although was badly shaken. But we had had enough, and felt it was time, to see a stop to the problem. We had prayed for safety. It was a busy road and you could have said, it was quite natural that there were so many accidents. However after more prayer, we discerned something deeper at work. We prayed and in Christ's name, broke what we discerned to be an occult curse, on that part of the road. There were no more accidents there, in the seven years, we lived in that place.

You may have a particular blockage in your church or area, where you are trying to evangelise, that is preventing a breakthrough. I encourage you to do some research, with the help of the Holy Spirit. Take a prayer walk around your area and ask the Lord to show you what you need to see. Ask Him if there is anything in the history of the area that is causing problems. Particularly important, are places where blood has been shed in the past – (Genesis 4:10) or where there is a history of covenants made with other gods (1 Samuel 7:3), or where particular sins seem more prevalent than normal. Are there places of particular occult activity in your area and where are they situated? In the church, blockages may include ongoing unforgiveness between members, or previous sin not repented of, especially if involving leadership. Generational patterns of sin – e.g., churches birthed in a split from another congregation, especially if acrimonious, often carry on a pattern of splitting. Other blockages involve religious spirits, or the influence of such things as Freemasonry, in the past or present. Churches may be targeted in prayer by occult groups.

We are told in 2 Corinthians 2:11 not to let Satan get advantage over us, by being 'ignorant of his wiles and intentions' and in Isaiah 62:10 to 'gather out the stones' as we prepare the highway for the people.

Let me encourage you to dig deeper about your breakthrough. Ask the Lord for His revelation to help you 'see the city' as it is, and to clearly discern the spiritual roots underlying blockages to breakthrough.

Key two - Sanctify yourselves

> *'And Joshua said to the people, "Sanctify yourselves: that is separate yourselves for a special holy purpose for tomorrow the Lord will do wonders amongst you"'.*
> *Joshua 3:5*

If you are desperate for a breakthrough in prayer, then the next step is to sanctify yourself, to become 'set apart' for that purpose. As we pray, we need to make sure there is no unrighteousness in us. We need clean hands and hearts 'to ascend the hill of the Lord'. If you are praying about a blockage and because of unrepented sin in your own life have a weakness in that area, then you are going to be in spiritual trouble, as you begin to pray. I am a local preacher and I know that often, when I am preparing for a sermon the Lord takes me through days and weeks of sifting, in the area I am preaching about. We cannot speak with integrity about something we do not live out in our own lives. In the same way, I must make sure I am not involved in doing the very thing as the blockage I am praying about!!

Setting myself apart – to see a breakthrough – may involve the discipline of fasting as well as prayer. Through fasting, we humble ourselves before God as we seek His face. Revelation can become much clearer in times of fasting. Those of us that cannot fast from food, for medical reasons, could try fasting in other ways – e.g. fasting from watching television for a season. It is amazing how much clearer we are able to discern, when we are not filling our minds with other things. It is interesting in this passage that we have to sanctify ourselves today, for what God will accomplish tomorrow. We need to have a heart in our prayer that is willing to get ready for what He is going to do!! Are you dedicated to seeing it happen, no matter what the cost?

Key three - crossing over the Jordan - Joshua 3:9-17.

The Israelites were miraculously led across the Jordan, into a new place. It was a place where their feet had not trodden before, and they needed to be led by the Ark of God's presence. There has to be a willingness amongst us, to be led into a new place of prayer – a place where we have not walked before; led by the presence of God. As we pray for breakthrough, the Spirit may take us to unfamiliar ground and teach us to pray in a way that is new. Let us be willing and open to His leading, not holding back because we have not been that way before. (Romans 8:26)

Key four – circumcision at Gilgal - Joshua 5:8-10

As we pray, we should remind ourselves that we are in a covenant relationship with 'the God of the Breakthrough'. Jesus tells us in John 15:7, 'if we remain in Him and His words remain is us then we are to ask whatever we will and He will do it for us'. Through our relationship of obedience to Christ we are His friends! (John 15:14) We have the authority given to us, in our position in Christ Jesus, and the power of the precious name of Jesus, as we pray. We need to understand our position in Christ and who He has made us to be, in Him. Ephesians 1:19 says that we have the same power working within us that God used in raising Christ from the dead. Our prayers need to reflect our position!! There has to be an understanding in the heart about this as well as in the mind. Do not let your prayers be feeble, but filled with the power of the Holy Spirit.

Key five - meeting with the Lord – Joshua 5:13-15

Far more significant prayer happens in five minutes, in the Lord's presence, than in hours of struggling in our own strength. Our prayers become passionate and have bull's eye accuracy. If we want to pray prayers that bring breakthrough, then we need to learn to soak in the Lord's presence, by worshipping Him and allowing His Spirit to touch us deeply. This costs in terms of time. Breakthrough comes through a life of intimacy. This is the place where God brings us the revelation we need and where we are called to enquire, "What says my Lord to His servant?" God will meet with us as we seek Him, for has He not promised to do so? He also brings us to the point of seeing beyond the problem to His purpose and plan in a situation.

I was involved in helping to run a 'Prayer School' in Guildford for a number of years. We prayed much for the problems in the town but it was not until we started to believe and pray for what we felt God was revealing about His future plans and purposes for the town that we started to see significant changes.

Key six – praying with the promise of God in your heart

> 'And God said to Joshua – see I have given Jericho, its king and mighty men of valour into your hands' - Joshua 6:2.

Joshua went into battle, with the promise of God in his heart. He knew that God had said there would be victory. It was from that place of coming victory, that he was able to receive the instructions for battle. We need to have faith for victory, in the area where we are praying for breakthrough: a faith based on the covenant promises of God to us as His children, not on the circumstances we see before us.

I was privileged to be able to minister in a church in Serbia, just two weeks after the removal of ex-President Milosjevic. I was there with the founder of 'Deborah Arise International', June Richards. God gave us a message to those hurting people. June spoke on 'There IS hope for your children', and I spoke on 'There IS hope for your city'. Everything in the natural, screamed that this was not so. God confirmed His word to those people that evening however, when He made a double rainbow appear right over the place where we were meeting. It was an awesome unforgettable reminder that His promises are 'yes!' and 'amen!' in Christ'. Seek God for a specific promise from His Word, about the situation you are praying for, then pray with thanksgiving and faith to our covenant God.

There were some very specific instructions, for Joshua to follow, to see the battle ahead won. God is looking for an obedient people, however strange the instructions He gives us may seem. There may be some stepping outside of our comfort zones involved, if we are to see a breakthrough. We must be persistent in obeying what He has told us to do.

For years I met with a group of Christian ladies to pray for the town of Dudley. We longed to see God break through, and every week we met in the dirty beer stained bar of the town hall to pray. Going into the main meeting hall, we would prophecy that one day it would be filled with prayer. Many were the times we questioned ourselves, as to what we were doing, and if we had heard aright. Eventually we moved to another town. Seven years later we saw in a Christian magazine that Dudley Town Hall had indeed been filled with prayer, for an all night meeting! What a joy! Be persistent! Keep going in what He tells you to do, even if you do not see immediate results!

Key seven – praise, worship and intercession together - Joshua 6:13

If anything is going to scatter the enemy, it is the sound of the saints of God at worship. God makes His presence known in the praises of His people, and the enemy hates it. Power is released as we praise God. He will break through barriers and bring healing and release into situations. There is an anointing that comes to a time of prayer when praise and worship are joined together with the intercession. This happens quite naturally in many churches, in other cultures. We need to learn from our brothers and sisters, where they are seeing powerful moves of God's Spirit in this respect. Time and again in the Bible, we read of stories of victory as the people praised God. Our prayers become more faith filled and targeted in an atmosphere of worship. We get to see our situation through God's perspective and become much more confident of His power to accomplish that which we are asking Him to do.

Key eight – do not touch the spoils! Joshua 6:18

The Lord needs those He can trust not to run off with the spoils of any victory - those who will not take glory to themselves in any way, for the coming breakthrough. He wishes all glory to go to His Son, Jesus. Can He trust you not to touch the spoils?

Key nine – the shout of victory! Joshua 6:20

Having followed carefully the Lord's instructions, the Israelites let out a mighty shout together, and the walls of Jericho fell down! The timing was perfect because they were following the leading of the Lord, and they shouted together in unity. Before this perfect time, the Israelites had been instructed not to make a sound, not to even utter a word. Be careful as you pray for your breakthrough, that you follow the instructions of the Lord. At times it is wise not to spread liberally abroad what you are praying by telling everyone about it. As they shouted together, as one man; it is important for us to pray in unity with others who believe for the same breakthrough. Find others who have faith for the same thing, or who you can trust to support you in prayer whilst you are praying. When the breakthrough comes, you will have a witness in your spirit that it has come. This comes as a sense of peace deep in the spirit, or a 'knowing' that the burden has passed. It was as the Israelites proclaimed the victory that the walls fell. When the timing is right in the Lord – believe it, praise Him and proclaim it, and you will see victory!

The breakthrough I long to see.....

I came to faith as a nine year old child, from a non-Christian background. As a child I had experienced much difficulty and sorrow as my mother was diagnosed with Multiple Sclerosis when I was just four years old. She rapidly became increasingly disabled, and unable to function well in a caring role. In fact, we children became carers, with all that this means, in isolation and practical and emotional difficulty as we grew up. Our family passed through many hard times. However, I had been invited to a club at a local church. At this church, this care-worn isolated little girl experienced a dimension of love that led me to ask questions. I became a follower of Jesus.

Even as a young child I would read my Bible and ask questions. My father once said to me that I asked 'why?' about everything and I do not think I have ever changed that in my life. As a child I used to ask God this question, "If things happened as they did in Acts, then why don't we see those things today?" God made a promise to me then that in my lifetime I would see revival and the things written about in Acts.

I have had the privilege of seeing revival in other nations, but the thing I long for with all my heart is to see a massive awakening here in the U.K. I believe we are beginning to see signs of change in this nation that give such hope – like the hunger for spirituality and the explosion of prayer, especially amongst the young. Will you join us in praying for this breakthrough in our land?

Prayer: Young and Visionary

Andy Frost

Andy Frost is a youth evangelist working with Share Jesus International. He heads up key aspects of their town wide missions and founded 'Dawn Patrol' a youth evangelism initiative in summer coastal resorts. He speaks and preaches across Europe, with a deep passion for young people to know God.

I want to see a revolution. More than that, I want to be involved in a revolution. I want what the dictionary defines as *'a relatively sudden and absolutely drastic change'*. To be more exact, I want a Jesus revolution.

Jesus was the ultimate revolutionary – his life was cocooned in controversy. His birth in a simple stable kicked off the most important revolution in history. As he turned over the tables in the temple, he seemed to be sparking a religious revolution. As he made his mark in the sand and showed grace to the woman caught in adultery, a social revolution was emerging. As he rode through Jerusalem on a donkey and people lined the streets, ideas rumoured of a political revolution.

And then, as his life was traded for that of Barabbas, an earthly revolutionary - and as he died a revolutionary's death on a cross and rose again - it was clear that his agenda was not of this world. He did not merely bring religious reform or social change. He did not even come to free the Jews of Roman occupancy as a political activist. Instead he came to revolutionise the core problem – the human heart. Jesus was dedicated to revolutionising the heart of the individual. This was his vision.

I want to follow that same vision. I want to live a life that provokes questions and demands an explanation. I don't want to be remembered as a 'nice Christian'. Nor will I be satisfied to be remembered as a 'good preacher' or a 'creative youth worker'. I want to be known as a Jesus revolutionary.

As Jesus spent time with the Father, so we as modern day Jesus revolutionaries, need to spend time in prayer too. Prayer is the bedrock from which we become revolutionary. The problem is that prayer has long been sidelined. Frequently characterised as quiet and boring, our prayers are too often sandwiched into an order of service between hymns. It is time to re-discover prayer as the way in which we communicate with the God who created the Universe. The only thing that the disciples asked Jesus to teach them was how to pray. His prayers captivated them and by no means did they label them as boring! Maybe it is time to give prayer a makeover in our acts of worship. Maybe it's time to pray a makeover in our lives.

As a generation of Christians, many of us are ready and waiting for a cause to die for. We have been sold too many empty promises. We don't want a vision based on materialism. We don't want brands to define our identity. We want reality. Until we have found something worth dying for have we really found anything worth living for?

We are a generation of pioneers. Perhaps, at times, behaving too much like Western gung-ho mavericks. But with the desperation of a depraved society and a post-modern mindset as the backdrop, we do live in exciting times.

As a generation we want to push the boundaries of innovative mission, deconstructing the preconceptions the world has concocted about this revolutionary Jesus. We want to challenge injustice where, for too long, evangelicals have by-passed the issue. We want to be at the forefront of the debate on new ways of being Church, defining new expressions of community. In short we want to take on the whole world and bring revolution to every aspect. However, this has often led to a hive of over-activity.

The sad thing is that in the midst of this plethora of over-activity, we can already see the casualties. In our earnest desire to see God break through, too often the first thing that goes is the depth of our relationship with Jesus. Prayer needs to be brought to the forefront and it must be embodied in the life of a revolutionary leader.

The busy schedules in which leaders immerse themselves are often a recipe for lives that are busier still. Without serious caution, we are engulfed in a cycle of churning out tired pre-packaged talks rather than seeking fresh revelation. Then when crisis hits, we escape reality with a two-hour dose of Hollywood rather than getting to the very depths of the issue.

We sometimes see the goals as more important than our relationship with Jesus and we try to do it without Him. In this quest to be young radicals, I see so many young leaders burning out, relinquishing their dreams or turning back to the world.

As Mike Bickle writes,

> 'It is one thing to want to be extreme or radical, but it is an entirely different thing to put that together with the heart of a love-sick worshipper. I know this from experience. You will burn out from being extreme if you don't have anything to fuel it. Encounters with God are what fuel passion.' (Relevant Church, p60)

This is my fear – that my generation, in its passion and zeal for transformation, will forget prayer. Prayer must not be missed off the agenda in our daily walks as we strive to be who we are called to be...

Prayer is the key ingredient in transformation. Like heat-quickening processes in a chemical experiment, so prayer acts as a catalyst that brings greater change faster. Prayer moves God to bring change. History is evidence of this simple process. His word is full of promises that when we humble ourselves and pray, the land will be healed.

We need to humble ourselves and take a reality check, learning from the lessons learnt over the distance of time. Each year I make journeys to places to connect with historic sites of prayer and build faith in my own life. Carn Brea is one of my favourite spots. The path meanders upwards from the car park leaving the 21st Century behind. Five minutes later from the towering Celtic cross you can stand and watch the shadows of the clouds chase their way over the green pastures of Cornwall interspersed with tightly packaged urban pockets. A place where primitive Methodists used to pray, Carn Brea holds something very special that time has not changed. As I shout my intercession from the boulders of granite that adorn the foot of the cross, faith levels slowly rise. It all begins in humility at the foot of the cross.

Recapturing how God has moved through prayer over the centuries is a real way in which we can build our own lives of prayer. And Methodism has, at its very bedrock, been drenched in prayer. 24-7 prayer is just one model of prayer that has been excavated from history. In the 21st Century urban metropolis, 24-7 prayer rooms have erupted into the limelight across denominations and ministries. There seems to be a pull in people's hearts to reconnect and rediscover our roots. It's time to get our buckets and spades and dig some of the spiritual wells that are rich in Methodist heritage.

Pete Greig, the leader of 24-7prayer, is one of my heroes. He is a visionary who dared to delve into the history of the 18th Century Count Von Zinzendorf and his prayer movement in Herrnhut. He then added a flair of creativity to resurrect this historic model of prayer that has now been brought to life for millions of people across the globe. Simple touches such as paint, poetry and music in prayer rooms touch something of the depths of individual's spirituality.

This needs to be the same for other ancient models of prayer. As we rediscover past styles and approaches, we need to include cultural hooks for today's culture that make it 'our own'. As I rediscovered Wesley's watch night services I wanted to bring to life that tradition for today's generation. What an important time of year as we thank God for what he's done and dedicate the New Year into his hands.

Eternal Echo was a New Year's Eve celebration of prayer. There was no planned teaching but a variety of styles and different rooms in which people could explore and discover prayer afresh for themselves. The styles varied from visual graphic exhibits, to Celtic liturgy, to African drumming, to creative art stations – all celebrating prayer.

The New Year's countdown began as some 300 teens and twenties prayed with deafening passion as a DJ blasted out a drum and bass track. As I watched the vision from Wesley's day transformed into the reality of today, I prayed that this would not be about one night but about 300 lives fuelled on relational prayer. That this would help to create an army of revolutionaries powered by intimacy with God.

I believe that as a generation we pray in some of the most peculiar ways and that this is such a clear picture of the diversity that God has created. As we begin to understand the width and breadth of prayer and as we connect with God, prayer moves from being the latest gimmick into a part of life's daily cycle.

As we diversify in our worship and prayer experiences, there is a need to connect with each other as Jesus revolutionaries. As relational Church emerges in these coming years, I pray that we will see much greater accountability, ending the cycle of "burnt out Christians" as we live our lives openly before close friends, sharing life's hurts and joys. As I sit with my "accountability mates", we play hot seat, allowing each other to question any area of our lives, from issues of lust to issues of finance, from issues of pride to issues of prayer. Then we pray for each other - prayer acting as the glue that links us as pilgrims sharing life's journey.

As we journey, these personal expressions of prayer become part of our life style. Time management is key to finding ways of slowing things down and escaping the frantic nature of modern life. I believe we will see more and more sacred spaces emerging as people find their own prayer hideaways – on a deserted beach, in a nearby park or sat on the balcony of their flat - their own "upper room". I hope that we will also see a re-opening of Churches 24-7 to accommodate people's need to escape and be with their Father.

In all of this, the key aspect of prayer that needs to be re-discovered is the art of listening to God. The number of Christians who have not been taught how to listen to God always shocks me. If we want to see Jesus revolutionaries shaping culture and history, then we need to help equip them to discern the Shepherd's voice. This is absolutely vital and as Church we need to start equipping people now.

As I teach the simplicity of listening to God, I am always thrilled to see the impact that it has on individuals. After I have finished teaching we always have an opportunity to ask God for words and pictures for one another. People are always amazed at how simple it is and stunned by how God can use them. In the next session, we take this new found gift onto the streets to share what God wants to say to people who are oblivious that God wants to speak to them.

Once people have learnt to hear God, prayer becomes not only the instrument by which we remain in Christ but it also becomes the tool by which we can speak prophetically into the world. As the Church rediscovers its prophetic voice, we will see more Christians at the forefront of issues of justice. It's time to take prayer from the safe confines of our comfortable services and back onto the streets. When the Church finally starts exercising prayer outside the confines of the building, it is then that we will see greater transformation.

Last summer as we placed a prayer couch on a busy high street, we suddenly saw the power of prayer. People from all walks of life who had apparently given up on God, had still not given up on prayer. What an opportunity to reveal Christ's compassion. People are intrigued by prayer as a phenomenon and we need to utilise this hunger for spiritual reality.

In the Church too there are people who desire to reconnect with God. As leaders today, I am becoming increasingly convinced that we spend too much time pointing out people's shortfalls rather than providing opportunities for them to come into communion with Christ through prayer. Perhaps if we spent more time pointing people to Jesus, encouraging them to spend more time with Him, they would naturally become holier, more passionate and more enthused. Intimacy will lead to involvement.

So we need to get involved as we pioneer in this brave new world but we mustn't disregard history as we explore fresh expressions of missional Church. We need to dig the wells, get creative and allow others to discover the richness of prayer.

So will you join me in praying for this revolution? I am praying that we will see not bones but an army. An army that will bring God's revolution of love to the UK and then on into the rest of Europe and then the World. Recently I spent time meditating on Jesus as the True Vine, and I realised just how key it is that we remain in Him. Without prayer I am dreaming an "impossible dream". With prayer, I believe that I can see these childish impossibilities come to light. Is this naïve? Perhaps. But I am still the child who reads God's history and sees the impossible made possible. I am the child that wants to start a revolution.

SECTION 2
SPARKING SPIRITUAL RENEWAL

Introduction
William Porter

Those who have been around the Pentecostal/Charismatic movement would think that spiritual renewal is an obvious priority for a congregation, but in actuality, for many, the possibility of profound spiritual renewal in the life of the church has not been on their agenda. This is a disturbing observation, given the declining state of many denominations and the challenge impacting our culture with fresh and living faith.

Martin Robinson, a leading British mission thinker, talks about the dynamic of *cheating history*. He argues that there is a sociological life cycle for a church or denomination. It starts as a movement, with great energy and inspired by God. As the movement gains force it attracts a lot of new people. The church grows by the addition of many new believers, and by its major inroads of the kingdom into its community or society. It then becomes institutionalised, a natural sociological progression. At that point it generally follows a path to decline, stagnation and death. But Robinson also agrees that it is possible to cheat history. What he means is that, at the point of institutionalising, instead of fossilising and dying, it can be renewed again by the Spirit to once again become a missionary movement. He notes soberly that many churches have not gone down that route, as history testifies, but it is possible.[1]

The challenge facing us here as a church is akin to the one posed to exiled Israel by the prophet Isaiah. In the middle of struggle, marginalisation and sense of abandonment by God, we are called to wait on the Lord to renew our strength, to soar on wings as eagles, to run and not be weary, to walk and not be faint (Isaiah 40v31).

1 Robinson, Martin & Smith, Dwight, Invading Secular Space (London: Monarch, 2003) ch 3.

God's people then were dislocated from their past and facing an uncertain future. Spiritual renewal is not a solution to polish up our old weary, out-moded ways of being God's people, but actually renewal of faith in God as worlds are shifting, and spiritual surge of courage to face a new future.

To put it fairly bluntly, many Christians need God to come and release in us again the life giving power of His Spirit. We are inheritors of many life streams of the Spirit in the last few hundred years, not least the Evangelical Awakening, the Holiness movement and, latterly, the Pentecostal/Charismatic movement. The latter, which is numerically the largest single current of the spiritual growth in the 20th century and indeed in the history of the church, almost defies quantification, so large are the numbers affected.[2] Yet standing in the legacy of these rivers of renewal, we have to ask God to do it again in our day.

The renewing power of the Spirit is two fold in regard to mission. It is a moral transformation within, and it is an empowering for witness outwards to the world. It's about both holiness and anointing. Randy Clark, author of 'Power, Holiness and Evangelism' and revival preacher says about the issue of holiness:

> 'I believe that many of us do not evangelize because we are so defeated in our own personal moral lives. Shame over our defeats keeps us from witnessing boldly to the saving power of the gospel. However, when the power of God liberates us, not only from the hell to come but also from the present hell of repeated moral failure, we cannot help telling others of our victory.'[3]

Yet, conversely, we also need the empowerment of the Spirit as individuals and church for mission. For, though we know something of what it is to be filled with the Spirit, do we actually have the anointing of the Spirit, that flows from a deep relationship with the Spirit, upon our ministry right now, one which will impact our

---

2 See Vinson Synan (ed), *The Century of the Holy Spirit: 100 years of Pentecostal and Charismatic Renewal* (Nashville: Thomas Nelson, 2001), esp ch 15 *The Worldwide Holy Spirit Renewal* by David Barrett

3 Clark, Randy (ed), Power, Holiness and Evangelism: rediscovering God's purity, power, and passion for the lost intro p4.

generation? As renewal writer and pastor, Bill Johnson writes about nurturing our relationship with God's Spirit:

> 'Those who discover the values of His presence enter realms of intimacy with God never previously considered possible. Out of this vital relationship arises a ministry of power that formerly was only a dream. The incomprehensible become possible because He is with us... It's the Presence of God that links us to the impossible. I tell our folks, *He's in me for my sake, but He is upon me for yours*. His Presence makes anything possible'.[4]

Many of us know about growing in the life of the Spirit (and that is a dimension of the baptism of the Spirit Jesus was going to bring), but how many of us know the powerful anointing of the Spirit upon us to minister breakthrough, healing, deliverance, salvation to people in need? Yes, the gospel lived and preached has an impact by itself, for it is the power of God for the salvation of all who believe. Yet there are times when Christians live in the faith-filled reality of that same gospel, and they demonstrate an increased anointing of the Spirit upon them for witness. That is what happened in Acts 2 v11 – the group of disciples were overwhelmed with a fervent desire to witness the wonders of God – they could not *help* themselves talk about Jesus! We need the reality of that anointing in our churches, to gain a joyful confidence in God once more.

One of the priorities of our churches right now, should surely be to help our people come into an experiential reality of life in the Spirit, not just in ones and twos out of a Christian holiday week, but spreading across whole leadership teams and congregations, from our ministry teams to our children's work, from staff meetings to church planting teams. We can expect the Spirit to bring moral transformation within and empowerment without - for healings to occur, for demonic deliverance, for addictions to be broken, for long standing problems to be sorted, for miracle conversions – the things we read about in the biographies of our Wesleyan and Primitive

4 Johnson, Bill, When Heaven Invades Earth: a practical guide to a life of miracles (Shippensburg PA: Destiny Image, 2003) p74.

Methodist ancestors. And this is what some churches and some ministries are already seeing happen in their midst. It is possible!

Spiritual renewal can become the catalyst for mission. It wasn't until the day of Pentecost that the disciples had enough and more to give away. The mission statement of a leading church in recent renewal says 'that we might walk in God's love and then give it away'.

Finally, to place this into wider church context, we hear the comments of William Abraham when he writes about the effects of the coming of the kingdom of God in church history:

> 'The coming of the rule of God through the work of the Holy Spirit is not confined to Pentecost and the early history of the church but is a dynamic, awesome, mysterious, active reality that sovereignty enters history again and again. It can sweep people along like a flood or fall gently like the morning dew. Either way it transforms human lives, creates a new community of forgiveness and compassion, brings new hope and joy into the world and fosters a deep commitment to offer oneself in service to the body of Christ. The church ultimately lives by such power and it ultimately grows by such power.'[5]

5 Abraham, William, The Logic of Evangelism: a significant contribution to the theory and practice of evangelism (London: Hodder & Stoughton, 1989) p100.

Experiencing Spiritual Renewal

Isaac Lim

Spiritual renewal is very much a part of the Wesleyan ethos. If you read the journals of John Wesley and the history of Methodism, you cannot but recognise that renewal forms an important part of the Wesleyan heritage.

When I look at renewal from a Methodist perspective, I am amazed at the richness of our history. The ministry of Wesley was a demonstration of the power of the Holy Spirit. His journal entries are full of stories depicting God's power and love. People were touched by the Holy Spirit, delivered from demonic powers and experienced healing in the name of Jesus. Hence the ministry of signs and wonders which we see in operation in many charismatic circles today are not new. John Wesley bore evidence of that in his ministry.

Some Methodist leaders get upset when they see people being ministered to fall under the power of the Holy Spirit. They say it is not part of the Methodist tradition. What they fail to understand is that the journals of John Wesley bear evidence of such manifestations in his own ministry.

The problem with many a Methodist is his or her ignorance of what is recorded in Wesley's journals. Many have not been exposed to these documents and hence are ignorant of their content. Furthermore, our leaders play down these passages and we do not get to read these texts. Our people go to independent churches and other denominations to learn about renewal when lessons on renewal can be gleaned from the journals of John Wesley himself.

I shall in this chapter highlight some of these happenings that are recorded in the journals of John Wesley.

The Aldersgate Experience

When John Wesley was touched by God at a meeting at Aldersgate Street on May 24, 1738, his life was never the same again. It was for him an experience of deep change.

In his journal entry of May 24, 1738 Wesley wrote:

> *In the evening I went unwillingly to a society in Aldersgate Street, where one was reading Luther's Preface to the Epistle to the Romans. About a quarter before nine, while he was describing the change which God works in the heart through faith in Christ, I felt my heart strangely warmed. I felt I did trust in Christ, Christ alone for salvation, and an assurance was given me that he had taken away my sins, even mine, and saved me from the law of sin and death. (The Works of John Wesley, Vol.18, Ward, p.249-250, 1988)*

The conversion experience of John Wesley was so powerful that it changed the texture of his ministry as a pastor, and catapulted him into an itinerant ministry that saw him crisscrossing Britain on horseback with the message of the gospel.

John Wesley's Pentecost

After John Wesley's conversion, another event took place on 1 January 1739 which is seldom highlighted. I would like to refer to this event as John Wesley's experience of Pentecost. This is what is found in his journal entry of the same date:

> *Mr Hall, Kinchin, Ingham, Whitefield, Hutchings, and my brother Charles were present at our love-feast in Fetter Lane, with about sixty of our brethren. About three in the morning, as we were continuing instant in prayer, the power of God came mightily upon us, insomuch that many cried out for exceeding joy, and many fell to the ground. As soon as we were recovered a little from the awe and amazement at the presence of majesty, we broke out with one voice, 'We praise thee, O God; we acknowledge thee to be the Lord.' (The Works of John Wesley, Vol.19, Ward, p.29, 1990)*

I do not think that when Wesley wrote 'and many fell to the ground' it was a figure of speech. I believe people literally fell to the ground. On recovering from that phenomenon, they broke out with one voice and said '*we praise Thee oh God, we acknowledge Thee to be the Lord*'.

Thereafter, the fact that his ministry was Spirit-empowered was more than evident.

The Power of Renewal as experienced by Wesley

Wesley experienced the power of the Holy Spirit in his ministry. People were convicted of their sins as he preached and some manifested states of demonic oppression. In the Journal entry of May 21, 1739 he wrote:

> *In the evening I was interrupted at Nicholas Street, almost as soon as I had begun to speak, by cries of one who was 'pricked at the heart', and strongly groaned for pardon in peace. Yet I went on to declare what God had already done, in proof of that important truth that He is 'not willing any should perish, but that all should come to repentance'. Another person dropped down, close to one who was a strong assertor of the contrary doctrine. While he stood astonished at the sight, a little boy near him was seized in the same manner. A young man who stood behind fixed his eyes on him and sunk down himself as one dead, but soon began to roar out and beat himself against the ground so that six men could scarcely hold him. His name was Thomas Maxfield. Except John Hayden, I never saw one so torn of the evil one. Meanwhile many others began to cry out to the 'Saviour of all', that He would come and help them, insomuch that all the house (and indeed all the street for some space) was in an uproar. But we continued in prayer, and before ten a greater part found rest to their souls. (The Works of John Wesley, Vol.19, Ward, p.61, 1990)*

Wesley's ministry bore evidence of the Spirit's Presence. Some would fall under the power of the Spirit in his ministry as well. In his journal entry of 9th November 1758, Wesley wrote:

> *We lodged at Mr Hicks's, the vicar, a witness of the faith which once he persecuted. The next morning I preached in his church again. In the middle of the sermon a woman before me dropped down as dead, as one had done the night before. In a short time she came to herself and*

> *remained deeply sensible of her want of Christ. (The Works of John Wesley, Vol.21, Ward, p.171, 1992)*

There are many other similar experiences mentioned in his journals.

What is Spiritual Renewal?

Firstly, it is the experience of being born again (John 3:1-21). We often use this term 'born again' when we refer to a person receiving Christ for the first time and experiencing a spiritual birth. However I believe this phrase can also apply to Christians in need of a fresh touch of the Holy Spirit. As the discouraged disciples were energized through the baptism of the Holy Spirit at Pentecost, we too need to be energized in like manner.

There are Christians who have backslidden or who have strayed away from the Lord or who have lost the enabling that comes from the Holy Spirit. They need to be 'born again'. Perhaps the last time you had an experience of God was a long time ago and you are in the midst of a spiritual drought. The Lord says, "You must be born again." You need a fresh experience of the Holy Spirit.

Secondly, it is an encounter with the resurrected Christ (Luke 24:13-35). Spiritual renewal has to do with a fresh encounter with the Risen Christ. You meet with Jesus and things change. It's just like the women outside the garden tomb at the resurrection of Jesus Christ. They were so excited when they met with Jesus. They were transformed. Paul says, 'If anyone is in Christ, there is a new creation: everything old has passed away; see, everything has become new' (2 Corinthians 5:17).

Who Renews?

We must say the Triune God renews – Father, Son and Holy Spirit. We know from Scripture that the Holy Spirit renews (Acts 1:4-8; Rev 22:17), Jesus renews (Matthew 11:28; John 7:37-39), and the Father renews (Luke 15:11-32).

God the Father, Son and Holy Spirit renews, transforms, and changes us. He makes us what He wants us to be. If we ourselves do not experience the touch of the Holy Spirit it is very difficult for us to communicate the same with others.

Personal Journey

Allow me to share my journey in the Holy Spirit. I have always been an evangelical pastor. I had my theological education in a liberal school, but I have always maintained an evangelical posture.
I believe the gospel to be the power of God for salvation to all who believe. I take the Bible as the inspired word of God and preach it authoritatively as the Word of God. In spite of that, there was always a sense of spiritual dryness in my life.

Something happened in one of our Methodist schools in the early 1970's. It was discovered that a group of students from the Christian Fellowship were exercising the gift of tongues in the school. The matter soon became a subject of concern for the school authorities and the church as speaking in tongues was never a part of the Methodist tradition.

As the subject of tongues became a "hot" subject, I said to the Lord one day, "I really don't know about tongues. If it's true that there is such a thing as speaking in tongues, I would like to speak in tongues."

So one day I went to the sanctuary of my church, knelt down at the altar and prayed, 'God, if there are "tongues", let me speak in tongues'. As I prayed, I began to speak in tongues. But because the experience was not an emotional experience for me, I quickly dismissed it.

Subsequently, I spent a year at the University of Aberdeen in Scotland and returned in September of 1978. On my return, I was appointed to Wesley Methodist church where the pastor had turned charismatic. I was appointed to be his associate. The first thing he wanted me to do was to assist him at the Power, Prayer and Praise Service that was held every Wednesday in the church. I tried to wriggle out of that commitment but was asked to bring my guitar and assist in the worship. The second thing he wanted me to do was to attend the Saturday morning prayer meeting held in the home of a lay person. Knowing that the prayer meeting was charismatic in nature, I asked if I could be excused. Again he reminded me of my position as the Associate Pastor of the church and that would require my attendance at the prayer meeting.

I remember attending the Prayer Meeting that Saturday morning. As we were praying I heard for the first time someone praying in tongues. I said to myself 'I can do that'. At the end of the prayer meeting, the lay people present asked if I would allow them to lay hands on me so that I could speak in tongues. I quickly declined the invitation.

One evening in January 1980, while my wife was expecting our second child, she said to me: "Isaac, can you speak in tongues?" Sheepishly I replied, "Yes, I can speak in tongues." She said to me, "I think you are bluffing. I've never heard you speak in tongues." I said "I really can speak in tongues." Then she said, "If you can indeed speak in tongues, let me hear it." Then I said to her, "if I let you hear, you must not laugh at me." So I spoke in tongues for her to hear and she burst out laughing. I was however to have the last laugh because the next morning I was awakened with her speaking in tongues. Up to that point we were not serious about the gift of tongues or things related to the gifts of the Holy Spirit.

Two months before our son was born my wife had a nightmare. She said that she dreamt that we were in a dark room and someone was pulling her hand. I told her in the dream not to be afraid as we were in the midst of a demonic attack. She tried to reach for the switch in the room in order to turn on the light but she could not reach the switch. She began to pray, but nothing happened; she began singing hymns, still nothing happened; then she decided to pray in tongues. As she prayed in tongues, the whole room lit, and she spontaneously cried out, "Praise God! Praise God! Praise God!' That was when I was awoken. I asked her what she was praising God for and she told me her nightmare.

Then she said to me, "I think we have been very flippant about the work of the Holy Spirit. I believe God is speaking to us through this nightmare. He wants us to know more about the Holy Spirit." I said to her, "If you think that is what God is saying, then I will expose myself to the charismatic renewal and see what I can learn from it."

That began my journey in the Holy Spirit. I began to expose myself to the charismatic movement. I attended all kinds of meetings and learned about the work and ministry of the Holy Spirit. I observed many things about the movement. I adopted the things I liked and rejected those that bordered on superstition and extremism. As a result of the charismatic experience, we named our son "Charis" when he was born.

The first thing I experienced as I moved in the Spirit was God's anointing. I had been praying for several months seeking God's release of power in my preaching ministry. I could prepare a good sermon, but there was no power in the delivery of the sermon. And so I sought the Lord's anointing. One Sunday, it happened. I was preaching on the life of King David. As I preached I felt waves of power go over me – wave after wave. It was a special visitation of the Holy Sprit. My preaching ministry was never to be the same again.

After the anointing, I began to see God moving in other areas of my life. I witnessed the power of God in the ministry of deliverance as people found release from demonic control in the name of Jesus. I began to see lives transformed and changed through the ministry of counselling and inner healing. I began to see the church grow from strength to strength as Sunday services were packed with people desiring to hear the word of God. The church was experiencing renewal. The church grew from 1200 strong to 3500 in eight years.

Why do we want renewal?

Firstly, we want renewal because it releases us from spiritual dryness. Ezekiel talks about spiritual dryness in the vision of the valley of dry bones (Ezekiel 37:1-14). As the Spirit of God brings life to dry bones, He can bring life to our lives as well. We need the refreshment that comes from the outpouring of the Holy Spirit.

Secondly, we want renewal because we need the enabling that comes from the Holy Spirit. God promises us the gifts of the Holy Spirit for the work of service (1 Corinthians 12:4-11).

Thirdly, we want renewal because we want our Christian lives to be strong and vibrant. When we are filled with the Holy Spirit, we walk in the company of Spirit at all times (John 14:15-17; 16:12-15).

Fourthly, we want renewal because we want to be used by God to do greater works. Christ promised in scripture that we, His disciples, can do greater works (John 14:12-14; Mark 16:14-18). I believe God allows us the opportunity to see greater works, as we minister in the power of the Holy Spirit.

We must experience the greater works that Jesus talks about. One area that many of us avoid is the ministry of healing. We excuse ourselves by saying that we do not have the gift of healing. We are afraid that nothing will happen when we pray and so we avoid praying for the sick because we do not want to embarrass ourselves.

Often we forget that it is God who heals and not us. If God is the healer then we leave the results to Him. Our duty is to pray. God's duty is to heal as He wishes. If we pray, some will be healed. If we do not, then none would be healed.

I remember going to the hospital to pray for a senior church leader. The family said that he was very sick but did not tell me the nature of his sickness. When I arrived, the family left the room, to allow me time to be with the elderly man and his wife. I remember not knowing what to say or pray. He was a dear friend of mine, an elderly man who loved the Lord and served the church and I did not know what to pray. Finally I asked if he would allow me to pray in the Spirit. I said to him, "Would you mind if I prayed in the Spirit? Would you mind if I prayed in a different language?" He said, '"OK pastor!" I began to pray in the Spirit. I must have prayed for fifteen or twenty minutes in the Spirit. As we prayed, the couple began to weep. The presence of God was so real. Several days later, he was sent home - healed. I learned several years later that God had healed him from cancer.

God wants us to have a fresh experience of His grace and love. Let's go for it!

How do we experience renewal?

Firstly, we experience renewal through repentance (Acts 2:37-39). God wants us to turn away from our wicked ways and trust in him.

The reminder from 2 Chronicles 7:14 is that 'if my people who are called by my name humble themselves, pray, seek my face, and turn from their wicked ways, then I will hear from heaven, and will forgive their sin and heal their land.'

Secondly, we experience renewal through the baptism of the Holy Spirit (Luke 24:45-49; Acts 1:4; 2:1-4). God wants us to be full of the Holy Spirit as Jesus was full of the Holy Spirit. We receive the Holy Spirit through faith. He takes control of us and fills us to the fullest.

Thirdly, we can experience renewal through the laying on of hands (1 Tim 4:14; 2 Tim 1:6). The Bible talks about impartation of gifts through the laying on of hands. It may be necessary for us to ask our pastor or the elders of the church to lay hands on us and pray for us.

Fourthly, we can experience renewal by seeking God with all our heart (Jer 29:13; Matt 7:7-11). The prophet Jeremiah says, 'When you search for me, you will find me; if you seek me with all your heart' (Jeremiah 29:13).

How do I know that I'm renewed?

Firstly, there will be a change of attitude (Gal 5:16-26). The fruit of the Holy Spirit will be evident. Love for God and for others will be the motivating force in all that we do.

Secondly, there will be a new experience of power in our lives (Acts 3). We will not only feel the presence of the Holy Spirit, we will experience Him in a fresh new way.

Thirdly, there will be a deep assurance of God's approval (Rom 8:16-17). Deep in our hearts we know that we are special in God's sight. We know that we dwell within the boundary of His favour.

Fourthly, there will be a hunger for God's word (Psalm 119:9-11). We want to know more of God and His will for our lives. We would want to study His Word and know Him more intimately.

Finally, there will be love in our hearts for those in need of the Saviour (Matt 9:35-38; 20:29-34). We will take the Great

Commission of Jesus seriously. We want to seek out our loved ones and share with them the message of salvation.

God wants to renew us and His church. Let us avail ourselves to Him.

A Recipe for Revival ..... with a dash of Chile

Rev Miguel Escobar with Mauricio Escobar & Andrea Benn

Miguel Escobar is international evangelist from the Chilean Pentecostal-Methodist church in Chile. He is the founder of Terraglobe ministries, seeking to encourage churches towards growth and revival. He is based in Florida and speaks and teaches widely, with a dynamic anointing for healing.

Introduction

If revival is about God visiting His people, touching their hearts and deepening his work of grace in their lives, then let us have revival and let us keep revival. For, when we are revived, we are truly alive!

What would it take to make revival breakout across the land? Numerous pages have been written, words preached and stories recounted of how God has moved in and on and through his people in recent times. The supernatural outpouring of the Holy Spirit in the last decade of the 20th Century focussed in Toronto and Pensacola has whetted our appetites for more. So many revival theories, models and formulas have been mooted. Yet in the midst of the shaking and roaring, the laughing and crying, we are still hungry for God to show us what we are missing. We still need the inspiration of the Holy Spirit to help us understand how to make the connections that will herald and sustain revival whatever it takes.

Could we find a model for revival?

Uncovering the stories of revival in different cultures and people groups requires a solid process. Where revival breaks out and God in sovereign power begins the process of changing and transforming individuals and the society at large there are similar ingredients and developments that have been in place. The historical accounts of revivals in the UK, in Wales, China, USA, Latin America and South East Asia complement each other and yet clearly demonstrate variations on a theme. Yet the ongoing revival in Chile, especially amongst the Pentecostal Methodist church, over the last 100 years is an untold story. As I have talked with Miguel Escobar it has become clear to me that the experience of the church in Chile is yet one more example of the way in which God is able to work powerfully with the inherent cultural DNA of the people group. If the recipe is revival then there are common ingredients which woven together bring salvation, healing and wholeness and make way for the Kingdom of God.

Why write this story?

So little has been recorded of the Chilean revival. Isolated by its strange geography and fiercely protective of its borders the Chilean people have rarely shared outside their own country the amazing things that God has been doing over the past hundred years. It is for this reason that Miguel has been keen to have this story written and read by the people who are praying and longing for revival. This then is a recipe for revival .... with a touch of Chile.

Hidden history

A church that began in 1907 with just 39 members became 1500 in six months. In nine years there were 15000. By 1960 the church had 40,000 active members and yet it has never been written about.

Even now one church a week is being established, perhaps because of the signs and wonders that continue to take place. The revival phenomenon of the early 20th Century is still active in pockets of the country. God is a healer and people are experiencing healing. Over many years of the history of the church the believers have seen it, heard it, and experienced it. Yet no Chilean national has ever written about revival and the church. Although there have been a few historical reports written by American citizens nobody from inside has ever shared it publicly.

Examining the raw materials

The revival in Chile is a historical fact. Huge numbers of people have come to faith. There have been healings and miracles recorded as God has touched the lives of individual Chilean citizens.

In order to better understand the revival process that took place in Chile it is important to unpack some of the elements of the people and the nation which make it unique. Perhaps the context into which the Holy Spirit began to move helped to shape and develop the revival experience. Before we can be certain of the ingredients and the result we must examine the raw materials. What is the Chilean palate? What is the Chilean taste?

Chile: "Un largo pais con una loca geografia"

Chile must be a leading candidate for the world's strangest geographical layout. Squeezed between the Andes and the Pacific there is a spaghetti like strip of land affectionately known as "the thin country". With coastline that stretches over 4300km (2700 miles) and yet never more than 180km (110 miles) wide. A total land mass smaller than any other South American country apart from Ecuador. Chile holds within its borders the world's driest desert, lush expanses of forest, glaciers and fjords. Back to back with the Pacific "ring of fire", Chile has 55 active volcanoes and 2030 lying dormant and earth tremors occur almost every week.

Often described as "the Latin American country that works" it is one of the continent's most developed nations with a robust economy. Strongly European in influence, known for their hospitality and creative flair, their attitude to business and the law has encouraged the label, "the English of South America".

Bordered in the north by the Atacama desert, where no rain has ever been recorded, to the east where the Andes reach heights of 7,000m (23,000ft), the glacial features of the southern most tip as it reaches towards the polar ice of Antarctica (where the land is only accessible by boat or plane), and the western coastline facing the broadest ocean in the world, the geographical isolation of this country has been attributed as the reason the Chilean people have developed a strong national identity.

Chile's principal wealth has always been below ground with rich mineral deposits like nitrate, the fertilizer ingredient that was once the basis of Chile's economy, and copper, of which it is now the largest exporter. Famous also for its wine grapes and for the abundance of other fruits, which thrive in the intense dry heat of the north, the southern parts of the country are predominantly farmed for grains and livestock.

The Jesuit influence

By the late 17th Century Chile was becoming more developed as a nation. The Jesuits brought over craftsmen, architects, engineers, sculptors, pharmacists, weavers and painters. They also collected the best library in the colony with over 20,000 volumes by the mid 18th Century. Chile was well on the way to becoming the prosperous and highly Europeanised country that would later be seen as an example to the more turbulent emerging nations of South America.

Opening doors

It was Bernardo O'Higgins who opened the doors for Evangelical Christianity to come into Chile when he invited James Thompson from the Bible Society in Britain to help restructure the education system. Without O'Higgins' influence it may have been many decades before Christians from outside Chile were able to influence this isolated nation, challenging the religious stranglehold of the Catholic Church.

An Emerging Nation

Throughout most of the 19th century, a strong state oversaw an economic boom which was concentrated in overseas trade and copper and silver exports. Chile encouraged European immigration and very soon German immigrants were controlling some of the larger and most profitable estates. The British dominated the shipping business that ran through Valparaiso, and by 1875 Britain was taking 70% of Chile's exports around the world, and sold 40% of Chile's imports. Yet Chile found it hard to compete with many other nations because the country is so far away from the markets. Coupled with this was the fact that transport and communication within Chile was still a problem.

In 1843 the University of Chile was founded and by 1860 primary education became a state responsibility and was made free to all children. Only 17% of the population were literate by this time but by 1920 the figure had risen to 50%. Today the rate of literacy is around 95%.

A New Century

By the beginning of the 20th Century railways were making travel easier and the towns were growing as industry boomed. The 1890's had been dominated by Civil War as the people fought to reduce the powers of the President but the peace time years of the new century were dominated by the fight for survival as it became harder to eke out a living in the countryside. Many of the peasant population were drawn to work in the nitrate mines hoping to escape poverty but they soon found themselves trapped earning low wages (paid in tokens) that could only be exchanged for goods in the company store. Disillusioned by poverty in a country where the police force and the courts were ineffectual many people soon realised that alcohol was easier to come by than fresh water.

It was into this arena that God began shaking the foundations of the people bringing a transformation to the nation as Revival was sparked in 1907.

The Missionary Influence

As its name suggests, The Pentecostal Methodist Church had been formed from the doctrinal tradition established in the heart of the Methodist Church originating in Britain during the 18th Century as a result of the ministry of John Wesley. The founders of this church movement had a sincere determination to see the church renewed and they were filled with the Holy Spirit in the same way as the first disciples of Jesus experienced during Pentecost.

Encouraged by this wind of change and anxious to reach a spiritually isolated people group the Methodists arrived in Chile in 1878. They were overseen by the North American Bishop William Taylor. Taylor gathered together missionaries who would come to live in Chile and help plant churches. As a result Rev Ira Hynes la Fetra, James Higgins and William Writh arrived spreading the Methodist doctrine in several regions and creating five schools. Between 1883 & 1884 the laws for lay cemeteries, marriages and registry were approved reducing the Catholic Churches privileges in these matters and removing the restrictions that had been put on evangelicals.

One of the most famous Methodist influences in Chile at this time was Juan Bautista Canut de Bon. Born in Spain in 1846 he arrived in Chile in 1871 as a Jesuit Priest but due to the influence of American missionaries he became a Methodist preacher. Juan was greatly anointed by God and, with Spanish being his native tongue making communication easier, he soon became tremendously popular. As a result of the words he preached and the demonstration of his lifestyle, many people were converted to faith.

A clean sweep

An American missionary Rev Williams Hoover, and his wife arrived in Iquique, a city in the north of Chile in 1901. They came to teach at the English school that was part of the Methodist Church but, led by the Spirit, they were soon pastoring and planting churches. In February 1902 Hoover transferred to Valparaiso to replace Pastor E Wilson as the pastor of the Olivares Street Temple and he began to encourage the church to seek to understand and experience the work of the Holy Spirit in their lives. This was to be a turning point in the history of the church in Chile. The Temple at Olivares Street had the largest congregation in the country and became known as the church where revival began.

In 1906 there was a huge earthquake in Chile. It destroyed many of the buildings in Valparaiso, including the Olivares Street Temple. The church were determined to keep meeting together and so they erected a tent, which became their home for two years before the temple was rebuilt largely due to Hoover's skills as an architect and the gift of $10,000 given by a wealthy donor from Chicago.

News travels fast

Although isolated by their geography and, at a time when communications were difficult, incredible revival stories from around the world were soon finding their way to the Christians in Chile. In 1907 Rev Hoover received a letter from Minnie Abrams in India. They had become friends during their days in Chicago and Mrs Hoover had discipled Minnie before she was sent out to work in

India with Mrs Pandita Ramabai. In the letter Minnie outlined specific details of the incredible work of the Holy Spirit that she had witnessed. She wrote about young girls in Mukti, India who experienced the presence of the Holy Spirit through visible fire in their bodies:

> "The Spirit was poured out on one of the seeking girls in the night. Her companion sleeping next to her awoke, and seeing fire enveloping her, ran across the dormitory and brought a pail of water to dash it upon her. In less than an hour, all the girls were weeping, praying and confessing their sins. Many of these girls were invested with a strange beautiful and supernatural fire".

Seeking the Holy Spirit

Encouraged by the incredible news of Revival the members of the church in Valparaiso decided to embark on a campaign to encourage the fire of the Holy Spirit to be poured on them. They began to meet every afternoon at five o'clock and, led by Rev Hoover, they held meetings that lasted for hours praying and praising God. As a direct result of these meetings manifestations of the Holy Spirit started to breakout amongst the congregation. There were tongues, crying, laughing, songs, dreams, visions, healing, and above all repentance, confession of sin and a complete surrender to the will of God. People began to be transformed by God's love and power.

The Rev Hoover explained this with the following words,

> "One might ask: What is revival? When we speak of religion we understand that those cold Christians become warm; those sleeping, wake up; the rebellious, submit; the lazy start to work; all of them encouraged by the love and Holy Spirit of God, which comes to the hearts because they invite it and give it room. The result is that many, who were not Christians, surrender to Christ and are converted to him. They see the power of God in their lives. They are moved by the same Spirit of God, in answer to their prayers and the activities of live Christians".

Manifestations cause reaction

In one meeting that took place during this time a member of the church began to speak in tongues for the first time and did not stop for two solid hours. The manifestations of the Holy Spirit continued to occur in people's homes when they prayed together. By 1908 the church members were calling for large prayer meetings with the people earnestly seeking deeper encounters with the Holy Spirit.
The Methodist authorities reacted against it. Considering these manifestations as an example of indiscipline and turmoil they attacked Hoover's leadership. On 4th February 1909, a few months after the first manifestations had begun, the annual conference of the Episcopal Methodist church was held in Valparaiso. The church authorities used this forum to further extend their criticism and accusation of Hoover's ministry. They commissioned nine presbyters to examine the case and assess the state of his church. By the sixth day of the conference the commission formulated a charge against Hoover citing; "Public and private teaching, propagation of false and anti-Methodist doctrines and seriously imprudent behaviour".

Baptised in the Spirit

On February 20th 1909 thirty-nine members of the church in Valparaiso met together to seek the baptism of the Holy Spirit. Disillusioned and disappointed to have met such opposition they cried out to God with great intensity and suddenly Rev Hoover was visited by the power of the Holy Spirit. Crying and laughing during the meeting he later described an experience of intense joy and "the sweet sensation of peace that can only come from a power encounter with God". He continued to laugh for hours after the meeting had ended and most of the group had gone home. That night he had a dream that 200 pastors would visit him in Valparaiso to witness and experience the Holy Spirit for themselves and to understand how revival took place.

Laughter and healing

On April 11th 1909 during a church service, members of the congregation experienced incredible things happening to them. The services went on for many hours and witnesses reported that "the faces of the people clearly showed the transformation of the Holy Spirit". People were laughing in the church for hours as they worshipped Jesus and as the Holy Spirit met with them. In the evening there was a Holy Communion service in which people were invited to come forward for healing. The Holy Spirit touched the sick and many were healed. Local people who were sick began to ask for members of the church to come to their houses to share Holy Communion and pray. The word was out in the streets that this was a place of healing and the people began to expect God to move in power. They were not disappointed.

A lady came to the church in Valparaiso one day with a tumour visible upon her head and in her brain. By the end of the message that was being preached at the front of the meeting the tumour had begun to ooze out of her ear and completely disappeared. A great conviction fell on the congregation that while the word was being preached there would be demonstrations of God's power. Healings took place even without the laying on of hands. All sorts of unusual supernatural events took place just because the people were meeting together praising God.

Reconciliation and forgiveness

The meetings lost all their formality. There was no set structure and the people were encouraged to be free to move in the gifts of the Holy Spirit and to be led by Him. By April 15th the Church began to meet in other areas north and south of the capital and the manifestations of the Holy Spirit were experienced in all the congregations. There was a tremendous reconciliation among ordinary people recorded as broken marriages and families were restored. People openly asked for forgiveness and salvation. The church members were spontaneously humbling themselves before God longing to be reconciled to Him confessing their sin and publicly repenting.

Despite all the internal politics and struggle the church continued to grow and the Holy Spirit was actively at work. During 1909 alone the church grew by 44%.

Sticking to the mandate

Hoover was determined to stick to the mandate that he felt had been given to him by God to see Chile transformed by God. Despite all the opposition he faced he told the new churches:

> "Our intention is to glorify God in our hearts and spirits which we give to God. To this end we will commit to work hard to save souls, not expecting to be successful, except for the blood of the Lamb and the word of our testimony".

Dreams become reality

By 19th May 1909 Hoover returned from a trip to the north to discover that the dream he had was a reality. Pastors from churches all over the country flocked to meet with him to witness and experience the baptism of the Holy Spirit. As a result the revival fire began to fan into flame across Chile with reports of people raising their hands and singing in tongues, praising Jesus in meetings that went on for hours with ordinary people finding faith for the first time filled with indescribable joy.

By August 1909 the church in Valparaiso that had started with just 30 committed members were reporting more than 800 people attending services every night of the week. Signs and wonders were reported at every meeting with praise and worship carrying on into the early hours of the morning. The people were coming back from work and going straight to the church building to worship with only a few hours sleep and snatched meals as they were so totally focused on seeking more of God. On 20th August many people claimed that while they were worshipping they were transported to heaven where they ate fruit of the best quality before being returned to earth. It seemed that the prophecies of Joel that Peter described on the day of Pentecost were being lived out in the experiences of these ordinary Chilean Christians. Reports were coming in from all over the nation of dreams and visions and extraordinary manifestations of the Holy Spirit.

Visions and angels

At this time people were recording their Holy Spirit experiences. These included laughing, crying, yelling, singing, special songs, tongues and interpretation, dreams and visions, spiritual transportation, trances and ecstasies. Many people claimed to have waking visions in which they were transported to beautiful places. Some claimed to have been taken to a special garden to speak with Jesus, visiting angels and confronting Satan. However, the most extraordinary demonstration of God's power in the lives of these Chilean Christians was to be seen in their lifestyle. The people who saw and experienced first hand the presence of God at these revival meetings were changed in ways that could be clearly seen by those around them. A new compassion was born among the people as they were broken by God's love. This could be seen in their eagerness to serve one another and to affect the community around them. People were filled with an increasing hunger to pray and seek God. Many were transformed as God healed them of addictions and destructive behaviour patterns.

Impacting the nation

People who had never set foot in a church building were coming along voluntarily asking to be saved. New Christians were suddenly being used to pray for others, to serve the church, to preach the gospel as increasing numbers were added to the church every day.

By September 1909 the public impact that this phenomena was having led several national newspapers to publish news stories which helped to spread Pentecostalism across Chile. Though many of the reports were positive, the newspaper 'El Mercurio' came down very hard on Hoover and called the Christians "lunatico". Hoover was accused of "deceiving, announcing his shams with shouts, crying and exclamations which could be heard four blocks away from the church building". But there were also those who defended the new work in Valparaiso and an anonymous letter was published in a weekly newspaper called 'The Chile Pentecostal' which described the positive aspects of Hoover's ministry. This letter outlined that: "souls are being saved, there are confessions, restitution and people abandoning their sin. People are going to the house of the Lord day and night to pray and there is an unusual interest in meeting together. The love of the people in the church for each other and for those of different denominations has increased and continues to grow. There is union among the members and new unity in families. There is joy in spite of great tribulations. God is greatly glorified because the blood of Christ is exalted and occupies a place of prominence. In addition never before has one heard of giving glory and honour to the whole trinity, giving glory and honour to the Holy Spirit. Never before has one seen such wonderful and miraculous conversions amongst the sinners of this country. New hymns and songs are being broadcast with great spiritual content and people are being added to the church daily".

Gloria a Dios

In September 1909 a young man, who was helping to lead a meeting in Valparaiso, had an encounter with the Holy Spirit. As the power of God fell on him he was filled with love and joy and he began to run around the church building shouting "Gloria a Dios" (Glory to God). After a while he felt compelled to run out of the doors of the church and into the street where he continued to shout "Gloria a Dios". The people were amazed. This sort of thing had never happened before. The congregation of 80 or 90 people followed him and began to join in, shouting "Gloria a Dios". He continued to run into a bar across from the church building where he preached the gospel. Once he had preached he ran out and went to another bar and another preaching the gospel. The rest of the church followed praying and praising God, and shouting "Gloria a Dios". Many people were saved that day and the church began to realise that they could not contain what they were experiencing inside the walls of the church but had to go out preaching to the people where they were. Though his name is not recorded the actions of this one young man who was willing to be used by the Holy Spirit precipitated the revival phenomena spilling out of the church to impact the nation.

They began to use the proclamation, "Gloria a Dios" as a battle cry in their meetings and out on the streets where they continued to preach the gospel. The 'Gloria a Dios' became synonymous with the revival in Chile and describes the flavour of the Chilean church that praised God in the face of the enemy and preached the gospel everywhere.

Conviction of sin

The people had begun to speak in tongues and prophesy God's word to the church and to individuals on a regular basis. The new phenomena they were experiencing meant that they were still trying to come to terms with how they should handle the gifts of the Holy Spirit, concentrating their emphasis on allowing God room to move.

Order and Control

By the autumn of 1909 the relationship between the churches was beginning to breakdown. On 4th October the Superintendent of the Methodist Episcopal Church (MEP) from Santiago went to Valparaiso to try to stop the revival meetings. He was determined to try to use his influence to stop the movement of the church in Valparaiso and to stop the manifestations of the Holy Spirit that were occurring. Desperate to bring order and control to a church that had grown to 1500 which made it the biggest single congregation in Latin America, he was most perturbed by stories that church meetings were often disrupted by individual members of the congregation being led to do strange and unexpected things.

In October 1909 the leaders of the MEC called on the USA Consul in Chile to stop Rev Hoover's influence once and for all, and they tried very hard to send him back to the USA. But by that time the people were experiencing the power of the Holy Spirit in the streets and in public places. People could be seen falling over and laughing in public places and in schools and colleges as the Holy Spirit fell on them.

Criticism

The secular media had begun to viciously attack Rev Hoover. Even the Christian press refused to publish articles that he wrote about the revival experience. There was a real battle to try to sideline what he had achieved in encouraging revival and he was accused of not submitting to the MEC authorities in New York. They were happy with the fact that people were getting saved and being added to the church numbers. But they had a problem with the style in which it was happening. The Rev Hoover had shaped and developed the largest single congregation in Chile. Yet he was now accused of teaching wrong doctrine to the Episcopal Church. Finally on Feb 20th 1910 he was asked to renounce what he had been preaching or be dismissed.

At this time, however, two new groups had emerged in Santiago. Seeking the Holy Spirit, and with a strong desire to see revival impact the nation, these groups had been consulting with Rev Hoover. Whilst the MEC condemned Hoover these new groups openly supported him and the revival he was leading.

On April 26th 1910 Hoover wrote to his wife (who had returned to USA because of the tremendous pressure that they were under):

> "Now I am free and I can read the bible with no limitation. The US Consul and I have become friends and he confirms that I am okay in mind".

However, Hoover did resign from the MEC in New York. This marked the end of the first stage of the revival growth amongst this young church, but miraculous and missionary growth were to mark its path over the next few decades.

Raising the dead

In 1926 a young boy who was 6 years old fell off a building and died of the resulting brain damage he had sustained. Witnesses were horrified to discover his broken body, realising that his brain was seeping out of his nostrils. It was no surprise therefore that when he was taken to hospital the doctors declared him clinically dead. His mother unwilling to accept that her son had died prayed for him to be resurrected and he was. Six months later he was completely healed. He could walk and talk with no sign of damage. Now an 85 years old, Pastor Sequel is still being used by God, and can be found preaching, teaching and praying for many people in San Antonio.

Missionaries sent out

During the 1920's The Methodist Pentecostal Church in Chile (MPC) sent out missionaries to Europe to preach the gospel. The MPC began to influence people in Italy, Germany & Spain returning to the places from which the original immigrants and colonisers had come from.

In the 1930's some missionaries went out to other South American countries, including Argentina just beyond the mountains, and soon stories were leaking back to Chile that Revival was being ignited wherever they went. The missionaries to Argentina took great risks as the relationship between the two nations has never been easy. Today 100 MPC planted churches exist as a result of the original mission from Chile to Argentina. Bishop Claudio Vera, MPC Bishop in Argentina, is currently building a temple for 3000 people in Bariloche (which used to be Chilean territory) with 80% of its local population being Chilean nationals. Bariloche is an incredibly remote place 2,000kms south of Buenos Aires and 3,000 metres above sea level, and takes 40 hours drive up mountain roads to reach it. It is a beautiful location and miracles have taken place there with great intensity of the Holy Spirit.

Hoover's demise

In 1932 the church split into two factions. Hoover was accused of serious charges and a number of the pastors decided to resign from office. Years later these pastors founded the Pentecostal Evangelical church. Faced with this situation Pastor Daniel Venegas became the first superintendent in 1933.

By 1934 Hoover was excluded from the church he had founded following acid criticism about his moral values. Tragically he died two years later, a broken man.

Umana's leadership

Pastor Manuel Umana had assumed leadership of the First Church of Santiago as a probationary pastor in 1912, as deacon in 1913 and as Presbyter in 1916. Following the demise of Hoover, Umana became the first General Superintendent from 1933 to 1950 and was appointed Bishop President of the MPC at the annual conference in 1933.

During Umana's time the membership of the church grew at an explosive rate. However, the idea was propagated that the beginning of the revival process was due to his leadership skills. This idea caused further division within the churches as supporters of Hoover opposed what they saw as a "rewriting of history". The Evangelical Pentecostal Church of Chile (EPC) was formed in June 1940 as a direct result of the disillusionment of Hoover supporters with the church that Umana was leading. There was open hostility between the two groups. That was not resolved until 1950 when MPC & EPC signed a peace treaty. Real estate that had been owned by Hoover, now the subject of bitter dispute, was shared equally between the two parties.

Revival continues

Despite the disunity between the evangelicals at this time the revival continued with worship teams being sent out across the country gathering groups of people willing to serve in practical ways to enable them to plant congregations in hundreds of locations. Their social influence continued to gather momentum, and by 1947 it was no longer mandatory to teach the Catholic religion in schools.

Mamerto Mancilla

Following Umana's death the position of Bishop President passed to Pastor Mamerto Mancilla from the city of Temuco. He proved so popular with the people that he was re-elected twice. He had been converted when he was a very young man after God healed him of a serious life threatening illness. After graduating in Biology he surrendered his life to God and became a pastor in 1942. During his 20 year leadership of the church numbers increased by more than 100% and 58 new temples were built dedicated to worship.

In 1984 Miguel met up with Bishop Mancilla and talked about the events of that time. Now 80 years old this respected church leader spoke to him of his experiences of revival and with a smile on his face he asked, "Do you see that window high up there in the church building?" Miguel looked up and saw a small window high up at top of the church building which was opposite the old man's house. "Yes – I see it" he replied. "They wanted to throw me from it – my own people, all because of ambition and pride. Opposition will come and sometimes it comes from those you have trusted".

Brokering an Agreement

Across Latin America church growth was also taking place in Argentina, Bolivia and Peru. The church in Chile signed an agreement with the Pentecostal Holiness Church (PHC) in Oklahoma, USA in April 1967 stating that members of the Pentecostal Methodist Church of Chile would be considered members of the PHC when visiting the USA and members of the PHC would be considered members of MPC when visiting South America. This gave both parties the right to speak and vote at conferences across the Americas.

Javier Vasquez

In 1965 Brother Javier Vasquez became the Pastor of the Jotabeche Church. Vasquez came from a wealthy family from the south of Chile. Since he had served as the official secretary for Bishop Umana for 25 years, the people voted him as a suitable replacement. Bishop Umana's widow, Mercedes Gutierrez, a pastor in her own right, was a great support to Vasquez as he took on the leadership of this growing revival church.

Twenty years later Vasquez was appointed Bishop President in recognition of the success of his ministry. His first decision in this new role was to decentralise the congregations, creating 17 sectors led by a Head Pastor who would have authority over the Superintendent Pastors of each district.

One of Vasquez's most significant achievements was the construction of the Cathedral temple in the city of Santiago, fulfilling Umana's prophecy. Using his own money to purchase the land on which the temple would be built, the church was then able to support itself with offerings and tithes being put towards the building costs, and the people pooled their funds for all the needs of the church.

When asked how all this was possible the Bishop replied, "Pastors love their churches and the churches love their pastors".

A New Temple

After seven years of tremendous work and sacrifice the Temple was inaugurated on Dec 15th 1974 at a service attended by high ranking Chilean officials. The church was now able to house 20,000 people, one of the largest congregations in the world. It is here that a National Thanksgiving service takes place every September celebrating the anniversary of Chile's Independence. Government officials and the Presidents of Chile regularly attend this service. Over the years this has included Augusto Pinochet, Patricio Aylwin and Eduardo Frei. The transmission of the services across Chile by radio and television has further increased the influence of the Evangelicals.

Services across the country attended by Governors, Mayors and other officials demonstrate that the tide of public opinion has changed. Where once the church was persecuted and marginalised the people now regard the Evangelicals as a strong influence and an integral part of the fabric of Chilean society. The number of churches has increased, the membership continues to grow, and the influence of the church is felt at all levels. Where once the membership could be classified as poor and uneducated there has also been an explosion of the Holy Spirit amongst the educated middle classes. The outbreak of the Holy Spirit in schools and colleges has enabled the church to reach graduates who have gone on to take influential positions in business and public life. This growing number of skilled professional people has enabled the church to develop programmes enhancing public relations, increasing communications, and sparking outreach in education and medical aid as well as providing a Christian influence in the arts, music and literature.

Going to the people

Historian John Alexander Mackay undertook an extensive study of the progression of churches in Latin America. He observed that:

> "It should raise grave, sobering questions in the major denominations of historical Protestantism that, in recent decades, the impact, growth and influence of the Pentecostal churches has been greater in the Latin American countries than has theirs. The reason would appear to be this: Pentecostals have not allowed themselves to become enmeshed in theological clichés and liturgical formalism, in ecclesiastical smugness or in organisational slogans. They have gone to the people where the people live. They have been sensitive to the people's problems and psychology. They have won a right to be heard by the people by what they have shown themselves to be by life and achievement in the people's interest. In due course they shared with people their convictions about God in Christ and the experience and power of the Holy Spirit". (Quoted in an article by Mackay, John A. in Presbyterian Life, 1970)

What are the ingredients of the Chilean Church today?

The people

At the beginning the church was only reaching the very poor and uneducated people in Chile. 80% of the congregations were made up of working class labourers and manual workers. But in the last 15 years there have been more professional and business people added.

The church started for those without hope and soon found the professional classes were just as "hopeless".

Today there are politicians and doctors and famous people. It was never a priority of the Chilean church to reach the rich and educated. Yet as the gospel has been preached in public places and Christianity has gained social respect in Chile many people in the professional classes are being added to their number.

Cells

All age groups mix with each other within the church and the Cells are not divided by age or particular friendship networks but by their geography. The believers meet in separate cells on one day in the week, but they meet together as one church every Sunday because it is good to be together. The concept of unity is very strong and people are prepared to travel up to 40km to get to the church meetings.

The music

The church services have consistently relied on the Methodist hymns inspired by Charles Wesley. There are 420 Wesleyan hymns that the people consider to be like prayers set to music. They have a primary purpose to bring people to salvation. Because the Chilean people believe that the songs they sing in church have been inspired by God they believe that these songs hold an anointing to see salvation, healing and freedom. As a result they sing the hymns with great passion. This intensity of worship and passionate singing is a key characteristic of the Chilean church.

There is some new music now, and in youth services the young people take over and do what they like, but in the main the new has not displaced the old. Some of the church leaders have said that particularly anointed Wesleyan hymns have been used to kindle revival in some areas. The young people still want to have new music and there is a need for balance between the old established songs and new creative rhythms. Not everyone likes the same style, but style is not as important as the content. If the songs convey the truth and lead people to worship Jesus in spirit and truth it does not matter what instruments are used and in what form they are performed.

Music is such an important aspect in people's lives that they sing everywhere. You can see them on the buses with guitars and on the streets in markets singing praise songs about hope and salvation, freedom and healing. The Chilean church sings more than any other in the whole world. They are not necessarily the best singers but just the most prolific. If you throw a barbecue someone will always bring an instrument. Song is everywhere.

The services

Describing the MPC services in percentage terms it is clear where their emphasis lies with over 50% of the time spent singing, 20%

prayer on bended knee, 20% hearing the word and 10% of the time given to inspirational & prophetic response. The services always start with everyone on bended knee and end the same way. Lasting between an hour and a half to five hours they just keep going if the Lord is moving and give lots of freedom to the Holy Spirit.

On your bike!

It is the only church that has a bicycle ministry team. The teams go out with only a bike and a bible. Every Sunday they travel over long distances to remote locations where vehicles can't go. Concentrating on the areas where the people can't get to church these teams have been known to travel over 1000km to preach in every plaza. Once they have preached they have grown to expect that someone will come out of the crowd and take them home to stay for a meal and offer them accommodation, and they are never disappointed. The Chilean people are known for their hospitality.

Respect for leadership

One of the characteristics of the church is an incredible respect for leadership. The people display a reverence for their leadership that has left them open for criticism. They do not call another member of the church by the first name but as a mark of respect they use the term, "Brother" or "Sister" or "Pastor". This same respect may not often be seen in other churches around the world. In Chile there is an incredible acceptance of leadership and authority. Much of this has been imbibed from Wesleyan teaching and is very much a part of the Chilean Church culture. Even when authority is delegated to others nobody will complain, accepting the decision and treating the stand-in with the same level of respect as if they were the original leader.

The dress code

The dress code is taken very seriously. Men must wear a jacket and tie like a uniform as a sign of respect, especially if they are going to play music in the church. Ladies have to be especially careful not to wear anything provocative, and will only wear skirts. It is not thought appropriate for women to wear trousers especially if they are to preach. Both men and women are extremely careful to look smart and well cared for no matter what the heat - and it gets really hot, especially in the north. The dress code culture of the church is seen as very symbolic pointing to the priority of God and the church in the life of the people.

The message

The messages that are preached at the meetings are almost always short and simple leaving lots of time for the worship. The main message is for people to respond for salvation and they consistently go over the same ground. But no matter what the criticism of the style or content the fact remains that people keep coming to the services. They have made a decision that every evening service must be evangelistic and they are very certain that this must not be mixed with teaching, mission or ministry apart from the opportunity to receive salvation. All services have an opportunity for testimony enabling the people to be constantly reminded of God working in people's lives on a daily basis. They insist that these stories must be no older than 72 hours so the news of what God is doing is hot off the press.

Personal responsibility for salvation

The essential ingredients for each service are freedom of the Holy Spirit, music, singing and shouting praises to God and evangelism. In one church in the south of Chile they are still experiencing 300% growth of the membership every year. Much of it is attributed to the way that the members have taken personal responsibility for seeing their family, friends, neighbours and communities saved. They encourage one another to keep up the momentum by saying, "Just invite your friends to come and have a good time and they'll come back again and again".

Discipleship

But with all the joy of numbers being added there is the very real challenge of ensuring that the new converts are made into disciples. The continuous emphasis on the gospel message has meant that the people are not regularly receiving teaching to deepen their faith and many are left at the point of their first decision to follow Christ, making the decision again and again, unable to take further steps.

Yet in all this the people are faithful and know with certainty that they are saved. They do not seem to struggle with keeping people in the church once they have made a commitment.

Growth despite the problems

There have been 14 divisions and splits in the church since the early Revival but even the difficulties have not stopped church growth. Each of the 14 separate divisions uses the same hymns and the same basic liturgy, retaining the same emphasis on preaching the gospel. The only differences between them are the faces, names and titles that they use.

The main problems for the church have come as a result of the ambition of individual people but each division has in fact led to growth. The divisions have allowed room for more people to be added and contained than if it they stayed as one body. It is a clear example of how, despite human weakness, God can bring all things together for the good of those who love Him.

Revival in Chile has been an imperfect process but better imperfect than not at all. In the words of John Wesley, "Oh Lord send us the old revival, without the defects, but if this cannot be, send it with all its defects. We must have revival!"

Using every opportunity

Another characteristic of the Chilean Church is that the people use every opportunity available to them. When someone dies they sing like at no other time, holding big services in the graveyards. The women go to the cemeteries to preach, laying flowers on the grave of dead relatives and holding services at the graveside. They focus themselves with concern that people understand Jesus and accept him. It is quite commonplace to hear that people have been saved at funerals after they have seen, heard and witnessed the joy and celebration of the Christians preaching and praising God for their salvation and eternal life. The whole church attends funerals as a matter of course, and the cemeteries are always packed out. Where once Evangelicals had to be buried in secret hiding places because of the restrictions of Catholic opposition, now the

Evangelical burial grounds have become focal points of their open air preaching strategy.

Priesthood of all believers

One of the most successful motivators has been that every member of the church is invited to prepare themselves to preach the gospel. They all understand that one day they could be called on to preach or to share their testimony and rather than shy away from this opportunity they have tended to rise to the challenge seeing it as an honour.

At the beginning of a church meeting the Pastor will point at somebody and say "Get ready – I might ask you to preach". Then when the meeting is underway he will point at the person and say "God bless you" and that is the signal to come forward and preach. More often than not the person will stand up and just repeat a bible verse or give a small story of testimony or a little message of encouragement as they don't tend to go in for long or wordy preaching.

From the very beginning every convert to faith called themselves an evangelist, seeing it as their primary goal to share their faith and see others saved. More than anything else the people put a big emphasis on the importance of bringing others into the kingdom of God. Reproduction of the church was and is top priority. People would always endeavour to bring somebody with them to church. Their multiplication principle remains that "if it's good for you it's good for them".

Releasing the youth

The fuel of every revival is the youth that are able to give a strength and passion that the church desperately needs. Young people are available, freed up and flexible and they need to be used, released them to preach, teach and share. The Chilean church have developed ways to make the most of the youth including them in everything that the older believers are involved in so that they can take an active part of church life.

Communion

The church only shares communion formally once a year at a special Communion Service held in November. The church leadership decided to encourage the people to prepare themselves during the year so that every individual could make steps to consecrate themselves and be ready to receive before they sit at the table of the king. Not everyone takes it; not everyone feels ready. Communion is regarded as a very solemn occasion. Some pastors feel that this practice should now be broken so that the local pastors have the freedom to call for communion when they feel it is right. What began as a good idea has become entrenched in ceremony and religious tradition. Inevitably breaking this pattern will cause more controversy and criticism.

Baptism

As a hang over from the Episcopalians the MPC have traditionally stuck to a sprinkle of water on new believers instead of immersion, and this has been a big drawback. New comers are gradually being given the freedom to fully immerse and the majority of evangelical churches in Chile are now doing this as a matter of course. In the beginning however there were no suitable facilities to immerse people and since the sea is very cold in Chile many used it as an excuse which resulted in bitter criticism. Yet despite the controversy over the amount of water needed to constitute a baptism God has used the 'sprinkle baptism' as much as full immersion, with people suddenly being filled with the Holy Spirit and speaking in tongues for the first time.

Alcohol

Although wine is one of Chile's most famous products, people don't drink it in church because it is regarded as a symbol of destructive lifestyle. Many of the early believers were set free from alcohol abuse and so it became church policy to use juice for the annual communion. Not all the Christians in Chile abide by this and though they remain happy to respect the weaker brother, being careful to demonstrate self-control and never drinking to excess, they have come to realise that this is one of those controversial subjects which is different in other cultures.

Careful language

With a healthy fear of the Lord amongst the believers there is an evident transformation in their humour and their use of language and a desire to seek personal holiness. This is not a forced or false thing but comes from an individual believer's desire to be more Christ like in their attitude and behaviour, and as evidence of a supernatural transformation.

Pride and arrogance

One of the dangers of dramatic growth is that it can breed pride and arrogance. It is very easy to become proud of the increasing numbers of the congregation as if the size of the church marks success in all things. The antidote lies in recognising that God blesses indiscriminately as we are reminded in Matthew 5v45: "sun shines on evil and good". The blessing of God does not indicate divine endorsement but merely reminds us that God is gracious and as a result we must give God the glory. Miguel is fond of saying, "Without God we are a crowd of people. With God we are a church."

Healing

Revival has sparks and one of those sparks is healing. Where there is revival anointing there will also be an anointing for healing. One of the primary reasons people are interested in coming to the meetings is because the word goes out that God heals. Stories of miraculous healing will always leak out and the people will come because everybody knows somebody who is in need of healing. There is nothing more dramatic to challenge a person's faith and understanding of God than to witness the power of God at work. When the sick are healed people come to Jesus. Healing follows the word, demonstrating the truth. The Chilean Church has made the connections between preaching the gospel and offering prayer for healing as a regular part of their outreach.

At the beginning of the churches history stories of healing became so common place that 85% of MPC membership testified to having experienced first hand the healing power of God in their lives.

A Ministry Team of South Africans travelled with Miguel over 1000 miles across Chile to churches asking, "who here has been healed?" Person after person could give testimony to their healing. The South Africans were amazed. There is 'a DNA' of healing through the population. The church has two strands - healing and growth. They go hand in hand.

Raised from the dead:

This is not an uncommon occurrence in Chile. One documented example is a lady called Maria Isabel Perez. Her family would often talk about miracles and these stories fascinated Miguel. They made no secret of the fact that Maria had been resurrected from the dead.

After suffering many serious illnesses Maria died at the age of 28 years. She left a husband and seven children. Irene was devastated. She was only seven, and her family surrounded Maria's deathbed and prayed for three hours. Miraculously she was brought back to life. Today she is a robust old lady and has gone on to pray for 4 children who have been resurrected from the dead. It was witnessing this incredible miracle that persuaded her husband Max to become a pastor and they served the church together until his death 37 years later. Maria still plays a large part in the life of the church, and is referred to as 'Pastora'.

Experience not head knowledge

As a result of the emphasis on healing if people are sick they don't wait to be asked. They get up and go forward for prayer automatically and church members lay hands on them. Often the people bend their knees as a sign of submission to God and many times people testify that their healing has taken place exactly where they are standing or kneeling without people laying on hands. There is no formula. Simple prayers are prayed without elaborate ceremony or fuss because the people understand the principle that it is God who is the healer. They ask expecting to receive. Another of Miguel's key phrases describing the attitude of the Chilean Church is "They confess it, express it and believe it." Sometimes criticised by others who are used to different cultures, their unique style and indeed Miguel's style is often to say the word and then walk away allowing God to do the rest.

Changing priorities

The stories of revival from around the world reveal that, when God is at work in the church and in the lives of individuals, people's priorities have to change. Though many may pray for revival to come inevitably there is a high cost involved in being part of a sovereign move of God that sweeps a nation, and not everyone is willing to pay the price.

For the Chilean Christians who found themselves caught up in the process of revival the shift in their priorities was very apparent. Led by the Holy Spirit they were suddenly thrown into new patterns and new rhythms. As a result the believers paid the price in their domestic life, foregoing their free time as they found themselves attending church services every evening and spending every spare moment preaching the gospel in the plazas or visiting the sick in hospital or in homes. Their willingness to serve and to dedicate themselves to bringing others into the kingdom of God has resulted in a strong church culture of commitment and preferring others. Many of the people sharing testimony at the services speak of the way in which God has enabled them to break free from self-centred, self-seeking attitudes and behaviour patterns to find freedom.

Impacting society

Historical revivals have always impacted the secular community. Alongside numerical church growth, miraculous healing and deliverance, there is clear evidence of God moving in all social arenas - impacting government and business, education and public morality and having a very real effect on law and order. Following a weapons amnesty, a museum in Santiago has on display a large collection of lethal weapons and tools of robbery handed in by men and women who have come to Christ. This stands as an incredible display of the impact of salvation on individuals and upon a city.

Regarding politics, six million Christians are a force to be reckoned with and the government of Chile has realised that they can no longer ignore the views of the growing Christian community when developing national policy. With believers playing an active role in government, and as key players in commercial organisations, the values of the gospel message are rooting deeper into the fabric of society. Two years ago the Evangelicals won the right to bring Evangelical Christianity into the schools and colleges, releasing the authority to educate the next generation to learn and find faith for themselves.

Challenges facing the church today

A New Testament concept for us to continue

The book of Acts urges believers to move in the absolute conviction that the power of God, through the manifestation of the Holy Spirit, is the only guaranteed way to reach the lost for the kingdom of Jesus Christ. Paul saw a statue to an unknown God in Athens, yet he was certain that he had committed himself to serving a God who makes Himself known and can be known.

At the beginning of the 20th Century the Holy Spirit manifested Himself in various points of the earth and brought about the beginning of a phenomenon called the Pentecostal revival. India, USA, Africa and Chile began to see spontaneous growth that was both unexpected and beyond the traditions and expectations of those times.

In Chile this brought about the creation of the Methodist Pentecostals from the Methodist Episcopals. A small band of 39 believers grew in one year to 1500 and in nine years to 15,000. Signs and wonders, proof of the unique and unquestionable power of God, were manifesting among the people. Healing of terminal illnesses and solutions to unsolvable problems brought large numbers to church services and many became active members of the church finding faith for the first time. Prayer meetings were lasting up to three days as the people became caught up in the presence of God. The Spirit of God provoked the people to laugh or cry throughout the services and even as they went home. The media came to witness these events and reported spiritual deliverances taking place. The outward manifestations of the movement were a source of great controversy in the social circles of the time as well as in the older more established churches. Things happened for which there seemed to be no rational or logical explanation which were not understood by everyone, but a sector recognised that it was a genuine move of the Holy Spirit. The church continued to grow in an enviable manner, and the spreading of the gospel has never halted even though there have been problems, difficulties and open opposition.

Contemporary historians have noted that the phenomenon of church growth in Latin America was spontaneous, powerful, and led by the Holy Spirit and should be recognised by the universal church. Brazil is undergoing amazing growth that is exceeding all the expectations of the most experienced and knowledgeable leaders of the church. Again in Argentina the things that God is doing are incredible. Men and women of God are being raised up as the congregations grow bigger than ever and miracles are being witnessed throughout the country. The statistics are quite overwhelming as thousands are added to the churches week on week and as church services are regularly held in football stadiums to accommodate the people.

The early church described in the book of Acts was a movement not interested in the theological fads of the time. The vocabulary of the believers was simple, sensible and practical, meeting the needs of the people. The message that was preached went straight to the heart of the matters that concerned the people. Ritualistic formulas were laid aside. The existing framework was broken as God was given space and time to move in the church and in the lives of the believers. The freedom of the believers in their ability to express themselves was totally new and outside the norm of the established religious traditions.

The ecclesiastical structures were exchanged for the guidance of the Holy Spirit. No longer were the customs and edicts of the existing church authorities binding for the believers. Instead each disciple of Jesus looked for a genuine relationship with the living God through the Holy Spirit. Most importantly every new convert shared their experience of Christ almost immediately. Sharing their lives they witnessed unceasingly day and night. The example of the early church believers and that of the believers in Chile demonstrate the biblical truth that there is "nothing new under the sun". The same principles of faith led to a massive growth in the church in Chile and can do so even in the current climate of different nations. It is possible that the simple ingredients of revival have been forgotten or overlooked by the contemporary church.

It would be unfair however to maintain that these vital ingredients are still present throughout Chile. Some churches have become so concerned about theories of growth that they have sidelined the dynamic truth of the gospel. Some remain cold and in denial of their need of God and the work of the Holy Spirit. Conversely, others have become so radical in their methodology that they have lost their Christ-centredness. Pockets of revival remain particularly in the more remote regions of the country. The manifestations of the Holy Spirit are still present in the majority of the congregations and news of healings and conversions continue yet without the same ferocious intensity as in previous decades.

The signs and wonders bring people to the church because they are curious to see what is going on. Growth is not growth if the people are merely onlookers. Dynamic church growth can only really be measured in the number of people who have their lives radically transformed as they surrender themselves to the Lordship of Jesus Christ.

The encouraging news is that where there is a void in the church God is ready to fill it. In the face of all the negatives the gospel has not stopped affecting the lives of ordinary people. God is still raising leaders with an incredible anointing to preach the gospel and see people saved, not just in Latin America, but as they travel across the globe exchanging their knowledge and anointing in order to impact other people groups.

The movement of the Holy Spirit that began at the turn of the last century is still very much alive. We hear stories from Africa and Asia of people being raised from the dead and of signs and wonders following the work of believers in Indonesia, Malaysia, China, South Korea, Japan and Singapore.

Miguel's calling is to encourage every believer to be involved in the task of reaching the lost for Christ. Mobilising resources in all places to reach all people groups from our own families, to our neighbours, our co-workers, impacting the communities where we live across countries and continents. If a band of twelve disciples could get the ball rolling we should be able to finish the task!

What God can do with ordinary people
Rev Andrew Baguley

Andrew Baguley is a Methodist minister in the Meon Valley Circuit in Southampton and has much experience of ministering in the power of the Spirit. Andrew has also been a key influence in the growth of the Alpha course in UK Methodism.

Everyone was amazed and gave praise to God. They were filled with awe and said, "We have seen remarkable things today." Luke 5:26

I suppose that if I was pressed to state a foundational text for this chapter then this one would be it. It is true that the subject is Jesus, the charismatic revival preacher and minister (Acts 2:22 "*Men of Israel, listen to this: Jesus of Nazareth was a man accredited by God to you by miracles, wonders and signs, which God did among you through him, as you yourselves know*.") But it opens up the possibilities for ordinary people like us to be used in an extraordinary way by and for the Lord. Having been involved in the thick of charismatic renewal and revival movements for the last 10 years, I can honestly say that I have seen some things that have left me totally in awe and wonder and on my knees. I have wept with joy and laughed with amazement at the wonderful things that God has done in the lives of ordinary people in local UK, USA and Singapore Methodist churches. It is what God can do with an ordinary person that blesses me in my ministry so much.

Of course the development of the above text in the gospel narratives reveals that God's plan is to use us in amazing ways for His glory. Another key for me lies in the kingdom manifesto (Matt 10:7-10):

> *"As you go, preach this message: 'The kingdom of heaven is near'. 'Heal the sick, raise the dead, cleanse*

> *those who have leprosy, drive out demons. Freely you have received, freely give. Do not take along any gold or silver or copper in your belts; take no bag for the journey, or extra tunic, or sandals or a staff; for the worker is worth his keep.* & 11:4-5 *Jesus replied, 'Go back and report to John what you hear and see: The blind receive sight, the lame walk, those who have leprosy are cured, the deaf hear, the dead are raised, and the good news is preached to the poor."*

This is spoken by the Lord, of both the ministry of the disciples and of himself. Whilst it is initially to the lost sheep of Israel it soon becomes the wider work of the disciples (Luke 9:1-6 & 10: 1-12). Acts 1:8 is another key, for here Jesus instructs the disciples and fellow believers to wait for power from on high. It is God the Holy Spirit who comes to endue ordinary people with extra-ordinary Kingdom abilities. We live still in the age of The Spirit and so we must both expect and operate in His power and with His authority to proclaim and demonstrate the kingdom is here.

It is not that we are limited by the gospel texts to what ordinary people can and will do. In the passion discourses in John's gospel Jesus teaches them about the central significance of the Holy Spirit in their post ascension lives. In amongst His teaching the Lord says a most extraordinary thing concerning the kingdom ministry. Rather than limit it to the miraculous work of the disciples and the 70 He tells them that anyone who has faith in Him will do all that he has done and even greater things because He is going to the Father. He makes clear that the post ascension or Pentecostal scenario is for even greater signs (John 14:12-14):

> *'I tell you the truth, anyone who has faith in me will do what I have been doing. He will do even greater things than these, because I am going to the Father. And I will do whatever you ask in my name, so that the Son may bring glory to the Father. You may ask me for anything in my name, and I will do it.'*

And now this brings us to the present day.

We live in a post-Christian multi-religious society and I believe that spiritually we are in a John 20:30-31 situation. My experience some 10 years ago was of many people being saved because of the power of what God was doing. Drug addicts and alcoholics, atheists and sceptics arrested in their tracks by either seeing a miracle or hearing of one.

I well remember one lady in her 60's powerfully touched by God with a healing miracle who, overcome by the glory of God, rested in the Spirit for some time in a meeting, before getting to her feet, quite changed. She had been coming to the Methodist church for over 50 years and had never seen anything of the power of God and had consequently never engaged in the reality of His kingdom in her life. I wouldn't say that she was not a Christian but she opened her heart to the Lord that night and received Him in faith as her Lord and Saviour. The transformation was quite amazing. She was not demonstrative and led a quiet life at home. Her youngest son was a fiery local preacher with an evangelist's heart. The next day on the bus to the city with her son and daughter in law, she paced up and down the bus, proclaiming to all what had happened and imploring them to accept Jesus as Lord. Anyone who knew her would have not believed that she could be the same person. Even her own son was embarrassed at her boldness! I cannot help but think of the woman of Samaria and her bold witness to the people of Sychar.

It is this type of witness and testimony that will impact families and local communities. Surely we are looking for lots of ordinary people who have been impacted and inspired by meeting the Lord Jesus Christ, to lead the church in its front line ministry. Church plants, parallel congregations, fresh expressions of church and workplace evangelism will only be a programme or hard work without a vibrant group of ordinary people doing extraordinary things in the name of Christ.

I want to stress too, that the extra-ordinary things are not limited just to signs and wonders and miracles, although like St Paul, I would love to be able to say that we have faithfully preached the gospel all the way from John O'Groats to Lands End with signs and wonders following (see Romans 15: 17-19). We need to see that

Tongue speaking ordinary Christians can also have an extraordinary effect on non-believers... (1 Corinthians 14: 21-25):

> *'In the Law it is written: "Through men of strange tongues and through the lips of foreigners I will speak to this people, but even then they will not listen to me," says the Lord. Tongues, then, are a sign, not for believers but for unbelievers; prophecy, however, is for believers, not for unbelievers. So if the whole church comes together and everyone speaks in tongues, and some who do not understand or some unbelievers come in, will they not say that you are out of your mind? But if an unbeliever or someone who does not understand comes in while everybody is prophesying, he will be convinced by all that he is a sinner and will be judged by all, and the secrets of his heart will be laid bare. So he will fall down and worship God, exclaiming, "God is really among you!"*

I well remember an Easter People meeting back in the early 90's at Torquay. The theme for the week was the gifts of the Spirit. During one evening meeting the Holy Spirit gave the gift of tongues to a number of people. A teenage girl sitting near me, who had been far from the Lord, was totally convicted by what happened and was fully restored to the Lord. She was transfixed in awe as a lady spoke out from the congregation in Mandarin. The message was interpreted by the speaker who was able to check the interpretation with a Mandarin speaker in the congregation. This Pentecostal sign was immediately followed by a man in the opposite balcony to us, who stood up and gave a powerful word in tongues which when immediately interpreted was a specific word for repentance to those whose lifestyle was dishonouring to God. The teenager couldn't take her eyes off the man; she said that she knew he was going to speak. As soon as the interpretation was given she broke into the deepest sobs of repentance that led her to the counselling room where her life was wonderfully restored.

The gifts of the Spirit are given for both works of power (ενεργαματα) and service (διακονια) and are given to ordinary people.

One gift that is often overlooked and which so many ordinary Christians use is that of intercessory prayer. If we look just at two examples from scripture we can see what amazing things result from intercessory prayer. Nehemiah and Ananias (Acts 9:10-18) spring to mind. My ministry has been dependent upon prayer and particularly the prayers of the intercessors in the church. I lost count of the number of times my spiritual 'exocets' would knock excitedly on my study window to give me some revelation or word of knowledge from the Lord. What a privilege to be able to minister with this sort of information.

I remember one day when one of the intercessors came hot foot from a prayer meeting to tell me that a young lady in the village, who had just become a Christian after a hard time on drugs and bad relationships, having found that she was pregnant, had been to the doctor to ask for a pill to abort the very new foetus. The ladies had been praying for the young lady and the Lord had shown them this and told them to tell me of her depressed and suicidal state. I went immediately to see the young lady and told her what the Lord had said. She poured her heart out and wept in repentance. She was awestruck that the Lord knew and had told us what no-one else but her and the doctor knew. She knew in that instant that God loved her. Her life was changed completely. She kicked out her boy friend and cleared the house of everything dishonouring to God. Now she is a powerful preacher with a prayer ministry herself! Another instance concerned a peripatetic hairdresser. She too was a low flying spiritual exocet. She would ring me up from someone's house to ask what to do as her clients were out in the Spirit under the dryers or on the kitchen floor. Husbands of the clients became believers because of her prayer ministry and the anointing that was upon her. I think that she brought more people onto the Alpha Course at that time than anyone else.

This radical transformation of ordinary people in both faith and action will bring about renewal of the local church and revival of faith in communities.

I believe that this is where we must be today. Real evangelism is about being on the edge. It is where people are vulnerable, lost and needy, just the people for whom the Lord came. It is real, raw and risky. That is why God does what he does with ordinary people.

An example of how God moves someone into this ministry concerns a young man, who I will call John. John was very involved with the church and although he wouldn't become a member, he was youth club leader and very popular with the young people, particularly the girls. He was very fit, athletic, good looking and single. Unfortunately he had not had the best of relationships with his father as he grew up. He was very repressed and should never have been involved with young people. God spoke to my wife and I about John before we arrived at the church to begin our ministry. Our prayer was that God would give us some proof of what we suspected. He did, very quickly and I was able to go and talk to John and confront him about his problem. He immediately put things right and stood down as youth club leader. We took appropriate steps also to effect reconciliation with some of the church families affected.

The outcome was wonderful. Within a year John had enrolled at Bible College, a forgiven sinner and new creation in Christ. He quit his professional career, gave his car to a very needy family and made his house available to a family who had just become homeless. John became, for a while, a local preacher in the Methodist Church and completed his degree in evangelism and mission. After Bible College he joined Teen Challenge and for a number of years poured himself out for drug addicts and alcoholics. I have great respect for this work because it is real and raw and risky. Jesus said *"From the days of John the Baptist until now, the kingdom of heaven has been advancing, and forceful men lay hold of it."* (Matthew 11:12). John's ministry and commitment have touched the lives of hundreds of young people. I have met some of them at meetings where I have spoken. When I think of John and how God healed him and has used him in a quiet and persevering relational ministry I am greatly moved.

God also takes quiet and sensitive Christians and gives them spiritual gifts and an anointing for ministry in music and song writing. We only have to look at the amount of new songs, inspired by the Holy Spirit since the late 1980's to see how many people are being used in this way. The Church is enriched by their ministry and at times musicians are especially anointed for specific aspects of corporate worship. One such aspect is that of the prophetic. Megan is a case in point. She was an ordinary member of a praise group in a large, fairly charismatic Methodist church. She plays the violin and is very talented. She is a quiet thoughtful lady with a gentle spirit. At a conference a few years ago the Lord spoke to her through one of the leaders and told her that she would prophesy through the violin. It seemed a strange thing to say but that is what the Lord said. She was to come out of the group at times and play on her own so that the voice of the violin could be heard. She would play in the Spirit and God would speak to people. Megan was taken by surprise and went away to pray into the word spoken over her. Since then she has gained in boldness and often will walk around the sanctuary playing the violin, stopping where the Lord leads, in order to play over people. The power of God's presence is tangible and the voice of the violin speaks and people respond.

I have a friend in America, who after he retired in his 40's as CEO of a major company, devoted himself to his love of playing the violin in worship. The Lord has done a similar thing with him and Tom will play during prayer concerts, walking around the sanctuary, stopping here and there. The effect is glorious. I have witnessed people being slain in the Spirit as he plays. I don't claim to understand why but I do know that his practising involves just playing by the Spirit in harmony or duets with worship CD's. It is so powerful. I am so pleased that he and Megan now have contact to encourage each other. They are, however, not the only ones with this ministry; Ruth Frazell at Toronto Airport Christian Fellowship is another. God has taken these ordinary people and equipped them for an extraordinary ministry.

You will, by now, have seen that God can and is doing amazing things with a variety of ordinary people. Not all callings and ministries are "up front" or "power ministry" but the results are equally wonderful through them all.

Personal renewal, in my view, often leads to God using ordinary people in revival ministry. The gospel accounts of ordinary people having an encounter with Jesus most usually end with them becoming great witnesses, and in many cases bringing others to Him for healing, deliverance and forgiveness.

It has been my privilege to see this again and again throughout my ministry. Sometimes I have met someone who having become a Christian years ago has dedicated their life to taking the Good News abroad. Ordinary people become missionaries. In one of my churches there are four significant overseas ministries. One involves a lady of mature years who has dedicated her life and ministry to Sri Lanka. She only recently retired as a teacher. She has single-handedly baked and made food to sell all year round to raise money for the poor and orphaned, the elderly and ill in Sri Lanka, irrespective of their religious beliefs. She has visited Sri Lanka at her own cost each year for 2 months to oversee at first hand the work in the orphanages, pre-schools, industrial units and with the elderly. It is an amazing ministry and the range of building and care work is staggering.

I know that this story can be repeated many times but it serves to illustrate what happens when God gets hold of someone and uses them for His glory.

God can and does do amazing things through ordinary people. The Angel said to Mary "With God, nothing is impossible". How true! So what is he doing with us?

Spiritual Renewal: A Work In Progress

Rev Steve Lindridge

Steve Lindridge is a Methodist minister based in Gateshead in Tyneside, where he serves as the District Evangelism Enabler for the region. He and his wife Elaine established the 'Mind the Gap' fresh expression of church in Gateshead for 20 – 40's. His heart is for future-shaped, Spirit-filled churches.

At a recent gathering of Church Leaders the question or statement for comment was put;

> "It has been said, if only the Church was spiritually renewed, we wouldn't need programmes for evangelism".

If only the Church was in better shape here in the UK we wouldn't need 'statements of intent', 'priorities and objectives' – we would be doing it all the time. However, like it or not, the main-line denominations, with a few pockets of exceptions, are in ever increasing measures of decline.

The answer given, was illustrated out of that old church choir entertaining ditty "And they all live in little boxes and they all look just the same".

The reality is we are not the same but unique, and though we all live in some sort of little box somewhere, we are the most significant thing God wants to use in our time today. It may be controversial to say we are God's greatest resource here on earth, but I believe it is what He wants us to know. Spiritual Renewal is the work of the Holy Spirit bringing faith back to life. It is God's transforming power at work within us.

Take this on board and consider that the sum of our individual lives touch literally a whole world of different folk who have no intention of coming through the doors of a Church building, yet these same people are spiritual beings. The Group for Evangelisation have recently published the results of an in depth piece of research, leading to a work on how do we reach contemporary spirituality in the UK. It is going to show that four out of five people in the UK today are not just spiritually aware but seeking. Albeit in mostly consumerist ways, with a significant degree of mix and match, but, and here's a significant big but, their spirituality has been identified by themselves as broadly Christian.

So here's the wake up call. They are interested in Jesus but not in coming to church as we currently know it. Therefore renewal in a place they are not interested in coming to might not be the answer. However, they will look at the genuine Christian's life and respond to our authenticity. We say what we do and do what we say!

Increasingly writers of Christian books are noting the change in values within the UK. A greater individualism, which distrusts institutions, dislikes authority and holds 'relativism' in a way in which we nationally used to hold 'truth'. All of these things are a challenge to us as Christians. Our faith is an expression of the truth we believe. We aim to live under the rule and authority of our Lord God. So what is God doing to equip His Church to meet His purpose, in reaching out to our contemporary society?

We believe in that lovely statement that comes out every now and then:

> "It's not the Church of God who has a mission but the
> God of Mission who has a Church"

If you think back a little, - no, not that far – we're only in our thirties...to what's happened in the last thirty years. God by His Grace brought the work of the Holy Spirit to the Church in the form of charismatic renewal, which blossomed and grew through the sixties and seventies, but became so often rejected by the main-line church and led to many house-church and other forms of church being established. More on that in a minute.

The visits of John Wimber in the 1980's started to see a gradual acceptance within main-line denominations of spiritual gifts and healing, but still much of the renewal led to confrontation and rejection within the established institution.

A catch phrase (pardon the pun) "on the Floor, in 94" started something that became "come alive, in 95", "the message sticks, in 96", "nearer heaven, in 97", "it's not too late, in 98" and "just in time, for 99". The Refreshing or Toronto Blessing became a talking point across the globe in all corners of theological reflection. Again it was soundly rejected by some, but many who initially would have described themselves as having perhaps a negative opinion, came, experienced and, although still questioning, found a very real experience that impacted their ministry for the glory of God.

Now in the 'naughties', as they are being affectionately known, we are seeing quite a different perspective especially within the leadership of the local church. Though there are still a wide variety of theological views, the clergy within my own area are increasingly open to everyday encounters of the work of the Holy Spirit. Healing Services are more commonplace and the number of small groups meeting in homes has begun to rise. The focus now seems to be much more on relational opportunities within which God reaches into people's lives and brings an encounter experience, rather than the big event. Although they still happen and the annual conferences are always a significant experience, many renewed Christians are simply getting on with it. They've had decades of input, teaching, and experiencing the work of the Holy Spirit, now they are being increasingly encouraged by God to get out and, in everyday life, respond to what God's doing.

It seems that finally we are not getting hung up on gifts and ministries but our passion is God's desire for His Kingdom to come. God's supernatural gifts (particularly 1 Corinthians 12) are for any time, any place, anywhere, in order to demonstrate the glory of God and bring His Kingdom a little closer to a few individuals. The roles we teach on in Ephesians are to equip 'the gathered' to go out! Why? 'For works of service' (Eph 4:12).

This increased openness to the Holy Spirit still has a long way to go in our established denominational church, but it is a very different place than we had thirty years ago. Although God has raised-up numerous effective churches through spiritual renewal they are only a plaster on a gaping wound in the UK today.

Two opinions for the future

1 - Kingdom connections

In our time and place I have never before seen and been part of a growing willingness across Church Leaders of all kinds to work together. Our common problem of decline has shaken many of us to see the reality of our sinful self-reliance and minimalist view of the Body of Christ. I know it's a very post modern view to deconstruct institution and reconstruct relational networks, but these networks, built out of a common heart and vision to see God's Kingdom come, are bringing significant change.

In this deconstruction I hear Bishops and lay folk talking about 'loyal rebellion' – why must we perpetuate what is ineffective in our institution? We believe we are here for a purpose but that purpose has been lost and we need to rediscover it as our main line work. So, effective work is being done in the 'breaking down of barriers and fences', parish boundaries are being crossed. It might not sound like much to a Methodist but it is major change for the Anglican.

Too often any work together has focused on our differences or political balance of contribution instead of Godly values and purpose. Money rules everything in institutional ecumenism. We have been so reluctant to give out of graciousness or looked to take back what might be ours. This lack of generosity has to change if we are to grow in working together to bring God's Kingdom. We need the gift of persistence. Yes that famous spiritual gift – written about by St. Paul in Ephesians 6: "Stand firm!". It's unfashionable and not glamorous but we must stand firm. So 'Stand Firm' against apathy, indifference, lethargy, ill-treatment and all the things Satan throws at Christians to stop them engaging in bringing God's Kingdom of heaven here on earth. So let us pray without ceasing – Your Kingdom Come, Your will be done on Earth as it is in Heaven.

2 - Journey towards Jesus

Established denominations will all but go to the grave as their funders die off or lose heart and give elsewhere (both these things are already happening in increasing measure). Unpaid – Tent-maker-ministry will become the workable pattern for Christian Leadership of the once denominational churches.

Increasingly desperate churches will turn from self-reliance to dependence on God. Ever increasing fresh expressions of 'the gathered' will be recognised as 'Church' and developed with linked strategies based around outwardly focused but very relational, small group networks, with a common aim – to journey towards Jesus. God has always cared for the individual and spoken specifically and directly to them but that individuality is not the end, but the beginning of belonging to the 'Body'.

This journey towards Jesus contains four elements of which our current church must take account of for the spiritual renewal of the individual, if we are going to effectively reach our generation with the Gospel. Much has been made of the first three by numerous works and the process or order they should be considered, in helping people become established Christians. 'Belief' is said to develop after the seeker first finds a fellowship in which they 'Belong' and in time their lifestyle values are transformed and they 'Behave'. To this it occurs to me is the fourth element of encounter or 'Blessing' when God does something amazing in a person's life, which brings a natural response from them to draw closer to God through this experience.

Let's view these four elements in picture form

Figure I takes the four general areas of beginning by which people come to faith in Jesus Christ and the significant thing is their movement towards Christ rather than away.

Briefly I will offer some content to each area.

<u>The Triangle = Belief</u>. It aptly denotes 'belief' born from origins of the Trinity. Many people come to believe in the truth about Jesus

before they actually know it through a relationship with Him. Grace Davies[1] and Pete Ward[2] have both worked on this dynamic of belief without belonging.

Fig. I "The Play-Station Model"[3]

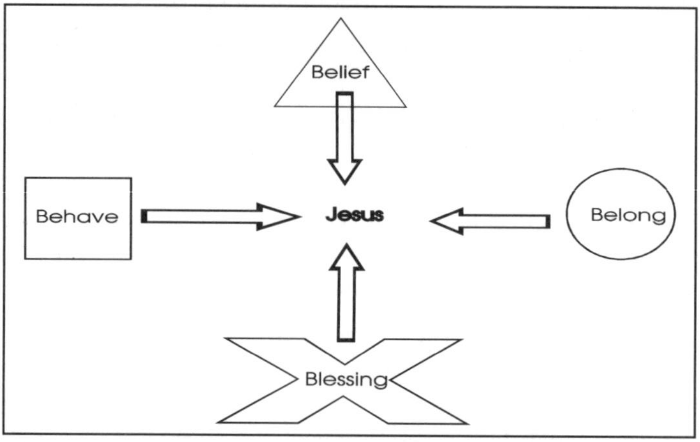

The Square = Behaving. How many times has the Christian been marked out as a 'square peg in a round world' because they want to conform to the Kingdoms way and not the depravity of the world's way? This approach is undoubtedly a smaller number statistically.

The Circle = Belonging. Many people find Jesus through a circle of friends to which they belong and as relationships strengthen so the individual is drawn closer to Jesus and begins to seek him for themselves. Belief, behaviour and relationship are often not part of many not-yet-Christians' value systems but they do like church and belonging to this group of folk who care about them.

The X = Blessing into Relationship. By the work of the Holy Spirit through ordinary and extra ordinary encounters with Jesus, people can respond to him with no real beliefs in place or belonging to a

1 Davies G, Religion in Britain Since 1945: Believing Without Belonging (Oxford: Blackwell 1994)
2 Ward P, Liquid Church (UK: Carlisle, 2002)
3 The shapes pattern correspond to a widely used video-game 'Control Paddle' of the Play-Station

group of believers, nor even be moral in their values and practice. However it is through the blessings they experience that God breaks into their lives; they respond and enter into a relationship with Jesus. Consider the woman at the well in John 4 and the concepts offered by John Wimber in Power Evangelism.[4]

Now I am not proposing that for any individual their journey towards Jesus is a nice straight arrow. I consider it much more a wavy line as shown in Figure II.

Figure II

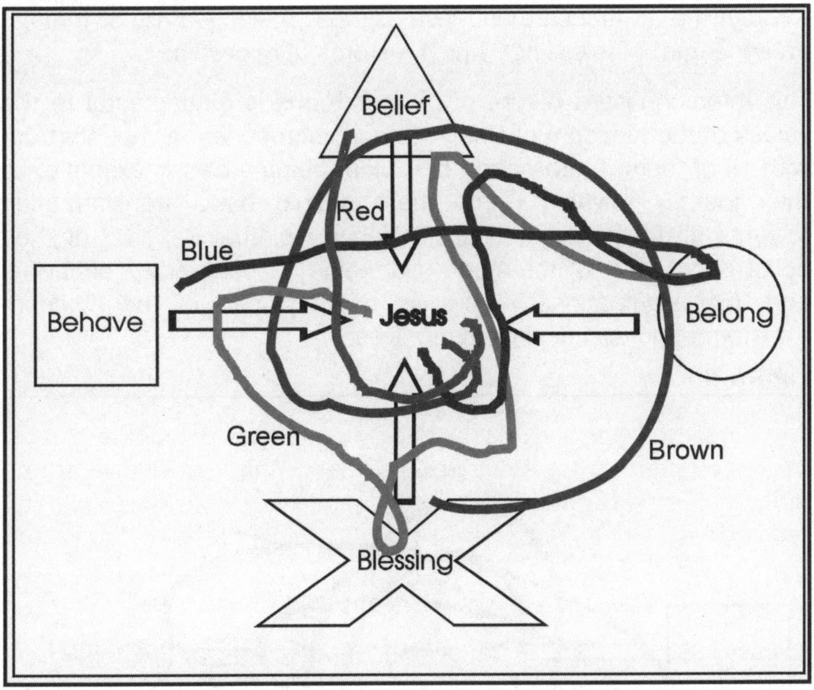

Life is never straightforward and our lives if mapped out, may indeed look very disorganised if drawn as a pattern. To illustrate; one Green line begins in 'belonging' then leads to 'belief', 'belief' leads to 'relationship' and 'relationship' overcomes or transforms

4 Wimber J, Power Evangelism (London: Hodder & Stoughton 1985)

'behaviour'. One could take any origin and map a person's journey of faith. It is a journey 'of' rather than 'to' faith because we in the west often incorrectly perceive conversion as an event or end point. Our death to me is the end point in our journey of faith in this life. So, Figure II illustrates the individuality of the path we take, yet the conformity to the essential elements or values of the Kingdom of God with Christ at the Centre. The closer to Christ we go, the more his values become our values. At times in our lives we may lose any one of these characteristics for a number of reasons, e.g. death of a close person leads to loss of belief – i.e. "how could God be real and allow this?" Yet, in time belief may be discovered again through the mutual care and love of those 'belonged' to, or through an encounter of 'blessing', which restores relationship.

This interconnected nature of all four terms is fundamental to the values of the Kingdom of God. Although someone may not start out with all of them, morality and behaviour being a classic example, as they journey towards Christ there should be a transformation towards all four characteristics. Hence Spiritual Renewal of their belief is only part of the story. Our value of 'belonging', 'behaving' and 'blessing/relationship' are as much a part of the Kingdom transformation God desires in our lives.

Figure III

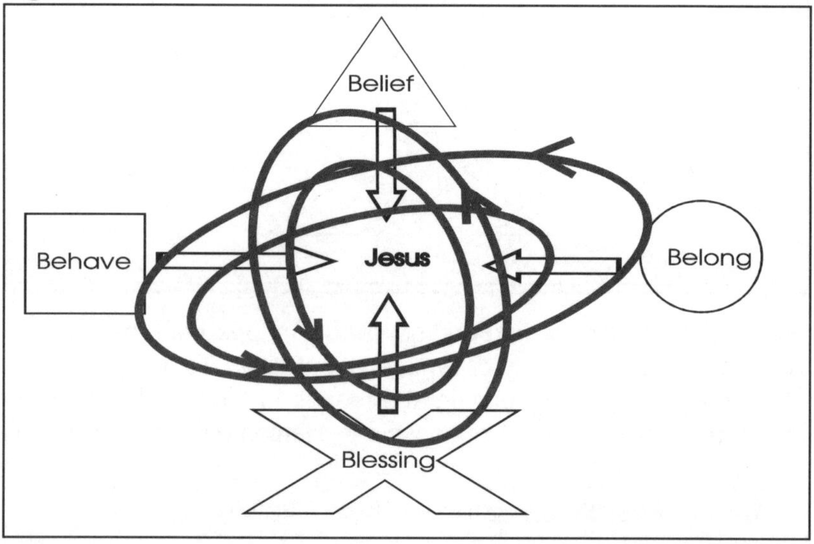

If I could draw a transparent sphere with Jesus as the Core of the Kingdoms values (white hot) and these terms at the four compass points, indicating the most extreme of positions away from the Kingdom's values (cold and black), then this would come close to explaining the context in which people could and do find faith. With this clear ball, one could see the journey from 'tepid belonging' to 'warm belief', rapidly moved on by a 'hot blessing', only to be cooled by 'bad behaviour' and then nurtured back to a place of 'hotter belonging and belief', resulting in becoming established close to Christ.

If we were to have a specific story for analysis, I would not be surprised to see a number of occurrences, instances, events, happenings, call it what you will, that had an influence for good or ill on the person's life helping them move towards or away from Jesus.

The application for 'institutional church' infers a vastly more adaptable attitude to the relationships between the four values. Especially when most fresh expressions of church are finding the not-yet-Christians being drawn in and getting involved at a practical level before ever being interested in faith – never mind the rules and regulations of being a member first and participant second.

It is every bit a challenge not to stand at some point in judgement of not-yet-Christians' initial odd beliefs, immoral behaviour, loose commitment in belonging and lack of relationship. However Jesus' first call to the disciples was not "thou shall not", but come follow me. This, for me, encapsulates where we need to be. Our calling is to come follow Jesus. The closer we get to him the more our lives are transformed into Christ's likeness. This is not permitted to those who knowingly profess faith but consciously deny Jesus by lifestyle. This is about being in a place of ignorance and the patience of the church lovingly taking a person on a journey during which their beliefs, behaviour, relationships and values of belonging are transformed.

Here's an irony, I started writing this at 6.30am Sunday morning the 13 March 2005 and at about 8.30 am Premier Radio was switched on where I was working. Rob Frost was interviewing Yvonne Richmond the researcher for the Group for Evangelisation into the

Spirituality of Contemporary Britain. Yvonne summarised the results and stated:

> "The Big questions of life refuse to go away – people are seeking spirituality and the Church must engage with them where they are."

That means going to them – not asking them to come to us. Jesus said "as you are going – disciple..." Matt 28:16ff. And if we take seriously the inferences of the Play station model, it will give us a much greater appreciation of how slowly people's values change and therefore how much more loving and less judgemental we in the church should be. Our challenge is in patiently nurturing them to maturity, encouraging them into ministry and equipping them for mission and service.

Our expectations and our strategies for discipleship and spiritual renewal should be put in the context of contemporary culture and reformed from there.

SECTION 3: RELEASING RADICAL LEADERS

Introduction
William Porter

We need to ask ourselves an uncomfortable question: are we organising ourselves to decline or are we organising ourselves to multiply? You can see the difference. One faces the problem: 'there aren't enough Sunday School Teachers. So we'll close down a class; we'll shrink our resources to match the decline. Or there's no one else left to run the next Alpha course, so we'll stop it now. It didn't quite have the effect we'd hoped for, so we'll channel our resources into maintaining our house group quota.' That's to organise for decline. To organise for multiplication is to say: 'we haven't enough people to lead our current groups. So we'll take a couple of people that we could use in maintenance mode. We'll pray over them, bless them, release them into a whole new area of evangelistic ministry. We'll mentor them to train up another six new leaders with their DNA, in the hope that over a couple of years God is going to bless us with a fresh harvest amongst the unchurched of our neighbourhood.' That's to organise to multiply. It's the faith risking kind of kingdom building which figures that, though we can't see it yet, we are going to channel our energies into places we can see God at work, and expect to see huge blessings in the future.

Jesus chose the Twelve, and the seventy two and the hundred and twenty. He chose intentionally to release them into ministry, even though the disciples couldn't see what was to come. He purposefully released new leaders into the harvest field.

What we're talking about here is an empowering-servant ministry, a ministry that knows 'I can't do it all myself; I need God to help me release others to do it.' We're not used to that, particularly our model of doing church, where 80% of the ministry is done by 20% of the people.

Dwight Smith, mission consultant put it this way in a passage relating to the effect of Ephesians 4 leadership ministries on the whole church:

> 'The outcome of leadership is always the same: Christ's people are empowered ... we could argue that this represents the minimum requirement of leadership and to that extent acts as a measure of whether someone is actually exercising effective leadership (italics mine).'[1]

It is what Wesley did, seeing the ineffectiveness of the Church of England's mission in the mid 18th century. His attitude was, in effect: 'there is a great work of preaching outside the parish system that I can't do it all myself. I will risk being named a dissenter and, though it will bring me into clashes with the establishment, I'll train up lay preachers across the country, wherever Methodist societies take root. It may be unorthodox, but the need of the hour is so great!' And so hundreds of circuit riding preachers were released by the early Methodist leaders to evangelise and catechise great swathes of the new industrial working class of 18th century England.

It is the kind of ministry that William Seymour, famed preacher of the 1905 Azusa Street revival embodied when he saw the potential of the fledgling Pentecostal blessing: 'this move of the Spirit isn't just for our little warehouse, it's for the world. And so I give all of you permission to become missionaries of the Pentecostal blessing all over the world. Even though none of you know more than the back streets of Los Angeles, you're going to go overseas and minister in God's power'. And so they did, naïve but radical missionaries and church planters, over twenty years, spreading over five continents.

It's the kind of faith of Korea's Paul Yonggi Cho who said, 'the Lord has shown me that He's going to build a significant church in Seoul. But I can't do it all myself, so I'm going to ask my male leaders to become my house group leaders. And they said, "no, it's not culturally acceptable". So I asked their wives, and they said "yes".'

1 Smith, Dwight, Invading Secular Space (London: Monarch, 2003) p144.

And so he started to build his new shape of church ministry with his women. He empowered them to make a difference.

We, too, need to model an empowering-servant ministry if we are to grow again. We must give ministry away, so that others can share in the kingdom work and be used by God. And this becomes the catalyst for growth. Fresh leaders become the primary tool in the hands of the Spirit for radical mission. The current vacuum becomes the ground for the kingdom breaking in. And how we need it. In Acts 6 this is precisely what the apostles said: 'We haven't enough people power to service this growing church community. So we're going to take the best people we can think of, and release them into whole new spheres of ministry, and see what God is going to do through them.' And the ministry of the church grew exponentially in effectiveness.

One of our problems within traditional church structures is that we fail to see, on one hand, the potential of our structures or, on the other hand, the utter limitations of them as well. The releasing and mentoring of leaders needs to happen both inside and outside our accepted ways of working. So, for instance, the possibility of lay preachers mentoring young evangelists and teachers. So, too, the potential of newly retired lay leaders to seed fresh outreach ministries within the recreational and social activities of the elderly in their area. So, also, the opportunity facing youth leaders of training up teenage small group cell leaders, from those who are starting to mature in the faith. So, indeed, the seed of hope embodied in a midweek alternative worship experience, as a church leader patiently trains up some new leadership of that event.

But the limitations have as much to do with our mindset as anything else – what we deem acceptable. And that is where we are so hidebound. Young preachers are seen as helpful tools for filling traditional preaching plans, rather than as contemporary communicators within their culture, and so are straitjacketed with administrative hoops to jump through instead of encouraging them in creative art and IT skills as a necessary medium for the gospel message. Fresh ministry amongst retired people from the church is seen as a threat if it competes against the past success of the ailing women's fellowship. Youth cell groups are seen as a marginal arm of a more important youth and children's ministry, rather than strategic fresh expressions of church. The alternative worship is seen as a waste of energy if it doesn't bring more people into Sunday traditional worship.

Most church leaders complain of a lack, not surplus, of volunteers. They wish they had more talented and willing volunteers to do what they would love to see happen in church mission and growth. Yet, in most situations, the true challenge is not the lack of radical leaders and volunteers, but the cost of identifying, recruiting, mobilising and mentoring them. The biggest cost is paid by the primary leader. He or she has to decide what to sacrifice in terms of personal ministry and church maintenance, to release fresh growth and potential ministries. Many of us have not been well trained for empowering servant ministries, and so it does not come naturally to us.

Yet, you see, putting opportunities for ministry and mission into the hands of others may be at an initial cost to yourself. But it doubles your effectiveness. And it releases people to fulfil their God-given potential, and seeds in them the potential for releasing other radical leaders in turn:

> 'Once your decide to invest even a small portion of the blessings God has given you into the lives of others, you'll find the seed of something powerful sown in your own soul. And someday, in the midst of giving yourself in the spirit and act of volunteerism that seed will blossom into the amazing realization that *this* is what you were made for!'[2]

2 Hybels, Bill, The Volunteer Revolution: unleashing the power of everybody (Grand Rapids, Michigan: Zondervan, 2004) p33.

Developing Radical Leadership

Isaac Lim

What is leadership?

Let me begin by defining leadership. John Maxwell defines leadership as 'influence'. J.O. Sanders first mooted this definition in his book 'Spiritual Leadership'. But leadership can be defined not only as 'influence' but also as the ability to get men and women to do what you want, because they want to. In other words leaders are able to influence people to such a degree that their vision becomes the passion of the people.

Radical leadership

What is Radical Leadership? I want to suggest that radical leadership in the Christian context is the boldness to challenge the status quo and to do what is needful to realise a God-given vision. The goal is not rebellion. It is to initiate transformation and change because God has spoken.

Radical leaders are often misunderstood. They are often construed as rebellious and non-conforming. As such, they need to be certain that what they are doing is Spirit-directed.

Radical leaders are innovators and pacesetters. They have the courage to be radical to realise a God-given dream. These are persons of maturity and integrity.

Jesus was a radical leader

Jesus modelled Radical Leadership. He did the will of God. The Pharisees saw Him as a threat, and tried to suppress Him. He believed God had spoken and sought to accomplish the will of God. A good example is the observance of the Sabbath. The Pharisees observed a legalistic view of Sabbath, but it was not so for Jesus. He was not afraid to work on the Sabbath because for Him, the Sabbath was made for man and not man for the Sabbath. If healing were required on a Sabbath He would hasten to do so. He observed not the law of the Sabbath but the essence of the

Sabbath. In this way he re-established the order of things to ensure priorities are right.

When Jesus spoke about leadership, he spoke from a servant perspective. He made it clear to His disciples that those who aspired to be leaders were to lead as servants. He demonstrated servant leadership by washing His disciples' feet,

His radical leadership expressed itself in His willingness to mingle with every sector of society. He mingled with the outcasts, the lonely, the tax collectors, the sinners and the prostitutes to the horror of the Pharisees and the religious authorities of His day. His focus was in helping persons enter the Kingdom of God and not shut them out. He was not against the structures that regulated behaviour in His day, He merely made sure that social structures did not deter Him from accomplishing His purpose on earth. He was in every way, a radical leader.

John Wesley was a radical leader

John Wesley was also a radical leader. When you look at his life you see the same leadership dynamic. A good example was his adoption of field preaching. In his days, field preaching was not an accepted form of ministry, but John Wesley under the influence of George Whitefield went ahead with it. The church authorities were upset with him, but he knew he was doing the will of God as people were ushered into the Kingdom of God.

Wesley organised his converts into cells within the Anglican Church. That too was radical. He began by organising his followers into little bands of men and women, then into societies of a hundred each, and then divided them further into smaller mixed groups of men and women called "the Class meetings". The Class meetings became the backbone of the Wesleyan revival.

Today, most large, thriving and growing churches adopt the cell system to cope with nurture, fellowship, ministry and evangelism. The irony is that Methodist pastors and lay leaders are going to these churches to learn about the cell system, when we have in our history the legacy of the class meetings. I believe it is time for us as Methodists to re-introduce the class meetings in our churches and to modify the system to meet the present age. Times have changed, but the uniqueness and importance of the class system remains the same.

The radical leadership of John Wesley was also seen in the appointment of lay preachers. He licensed laypersons to preach and teach in his movement. They became an important ingredient in sustaining the Wesleyan revival.

Radical leaders understand the texture of biblical leadership

There are three pillars of biblical leadership that are important for us to take cognizance of as we consider radical leadership.

Firstly, Biblical leadership is spiritual. It is spiritual because God is Spirit. They that worship Him must worship Him in spirit and in truth. Hence a Biblical Leader is Spirit-directed, Spirit-empowered and Spirit-enabled.

As Christian leaders we recognise that the source of our strength is not ourselves or our personality but the baptism of the Holy Spirit. To me, the baptism of the Holy Spirit is crucial.

The word "baptism" comes from the Greek word *'baptizo'* which means to be immersed or submerged. It is likened to a sunken ship that is totally immersed in water. When a ship is totally submerged we say that the ship has water and the water has the ship. It is the same with being baptised in the Holy Spirit. When we are baptised in the Holy Spirit, we have the Holy Spirit, and the Holy Spirit has us. In other words, we are full of the Holy Spirit.

If we are baptised in the Holy Spirit invariably all the gifts of the Holy Spirit are available for us. God may not endow us with all the gifts, but they are available for the church. Hence, will all speak in tongues? No! Will all minister healing? No! Can some be endowed with healing gifts? Of course they can! Can some pray in tongues? Of course they can! God will give the church the variety of gifts to enable the church to function as a body.

Jesus Himself was baptised in the Holy Spirit at the very outset of His ministry. The Bible tells us that Jesus was full of the Holy Spirit.

This phrase 'full of the Holy Spirit' first appears in Luke 4:1 and again in Luke 4:14. Jesus affirms His Spirit baptism in Luke 4:18 where he says 'the Spirit of the Lord is upon me because He has anointed me to bring the good news to the poor, He has sent me to proclaim release of the captives and recovery of sight to the blind, to let the oppressed go free, to proclaim the year of the Lord's favour'.

I believe that if we are to be radical leaders, with a desire to make a difference, we must be baptised in the Holy Spirit. The Holy Spirit not only enables us, He also guides and directs us. Spiritual leaders know what it means to be Spirit directed. The Apostle Paul was such a person. If you read the life of Paul, you will find him sensitive to the promptings of the Holy Spirit. In Acts 16:6-10, when doors were closed for Asia, they were redirected by the Spirit to Macedonia instead.

Radical Leaders are anointed leaders. Jesus is known as the anointed one. The word "*christos*" means "the anointed one". If Jesus, the Son of God needed to be anointed by the Holy Spirit, we who are God's servants need also the anointing, the empowering, the infilling of the Holy Spirit. The anointing was an act of God and the word was used metaphorically to mean the bestowal of divine favour.

Anointing in the Old Testament was the pouring of oil on a person and allowing it to flow down his body to his feet (Psalm 23:5; Psalm 92:10). It was an appointment to a special function. As we look at the life of David, we note that he too was anointed with oil. We are told in 1 Samuel 16:13 that 'Samuel took the horn of oil and anointed him in the presence of his brothers and the Spirit of the Lord came mightily upon David from that day forward.' There was a powerful anointing of the Spirit on David's life. The same can be said of Spirit-anointed leaders today.

Secondly, Biblical leadership is service-oriented. Biblical leadership is not only spiritual it is also service oriented. Hence a Biblical leader is also a servant leader.

In Luke 22:24-34, Jesus highlights the importance of servanthood when He addresses the issue of greatness. Jesus reminded His disciples that they were to be servants first. In John 13:3-15, Jesus again emphasized the importance of servant leadership when He washed the disciples' feet. He said to the disciples, "So if I, your Lord and Teacher, have washed your feet, you also ought to wash one another's feet" (John 13:14).

Paul highlights the servant disposition of Jesus in Philippians 2:5-11. Jesus is here exalted because of His willingness to serve. A servant leader derives his authority from his service. You honour a pastor who works hard, because you know that he loves you and he demonstrates this by his service. Jesus demonstrated the same by His life. I believe that God calls us to be servants first and then leaders.

Thirdly, Biblical leadership is life transforming. Biblical leaders are change agents.

When we talk about conversion, we talk about multifaceted change. I believe the conversion of the soul must issue forth in the conversion of ecology, the conversion of economy, the conversion of culture and the conversion of society. If a person comes to know Christ something happens to him that compels him also to effect change in his environment. His work ethic changes and this affects not only him but also those around him. His concern for the environment also changes. He recognises that life is about people and that he has a responsibility to improve his environment for the sake of his community.

It is for this reason that churches are involved in social outreach to the community. They recognise that the conversion of the soul must lead also to the conversion of society and ecology. Christians become change agents.

Some people don't like conversion because they know that the old will pass away and the new will come, and they don't like that. When people stop drinking, that is not good for the alcohol industry. Conversion will affect society and that is the radical part of renewal.

The life of Paul demonstrates this. When Paul encountered Christ on the road to Damascus, he was never the same again. He accepted his call to minister to the gentiles (Acts 9:15) and wherever he went communities were transformed. In Ephesus a major riot broke out because of the effectiveness of his ministry (Acts 19). Paul believed in the doctrine of the 'new creation' (2 Corinthians 5:17). He believed that a person is re-created when Christ resides in his or her life as Lord and Saviour.

Radical leaders understand the price of leadership

Firstly, Radical leaders understand the meaning of the basin and the towel (John 13:1-20). They understand the price of leadership. They understand that leadership is service and not position; it is ministry and not politics; it is the giving of ourselves, our resources, our family and not just receiving. I am not saying that we cannot receive a blessing that comes as a result of service; receiving is good but the starting point is always the giving of ourselves in service (Mark 10:42-44).

I teach Christian leaders "motivation" and I tell them that there is a difference between Christian motivation and secular motivation. Secular motivation is self-centred. Here, people are motivated by what they can gain. It is not so with Biblical motivation. Here, the Christian is motivated by what he or she can give. It is not what you can get because you have already received the best in Christ - the gift of eternal life. So the question you ask is 'what can I give? How can I bless the community? How can I bless the church? How can I bless another person?' We are motivated by what God wants us to do. The call, the commission, and the mandate drive us to become the people God wants us to be.

Secondly, Radical leaders understand the challenges of the Cross (Luke 14:25-33; 23:26-49). The cross is the difficult part of the Christian life. Whilst we talk about a God who loves and cares for us, we must also remember that the pathway of Jesus is the pathway of the cross. There may be times when God would require us to carry the cross and suffer for His sake. Perhaps some of us might end up being nailed to the cross of pain and shame. Would we be ready for that (Matt 20:20-27)?

If you want to be a radical, you must expect such a possibility. But God has a strange way of turning things around. Through the experience of the cross comes the resurrection. Through the experience of pain, you get to see the glory of God.

I once went through a very difficult time in my ministry. In the second year of my term as President of the Trinity Annual Conference anonymous letters were sent to hundreds of church leaders and national leaders with the view of staining my character. I was accused of things I never did. Over flimsy evidence, I was put on charge through the church's judicial system not once but twice. The ordeal lasted three years. However, the hand of God was over me to protect and preserve. I was found innocent of all charges and had the privilege of serving three terms as President completing a total of twelve years in the same office (the maximum one can serve).

Thirdly, Radical leaders understand 'Gethsemane' (Matt 26:26-56). Radical Leaders go through many Gethsemane moments in their lives. These are moments when we bring our deepest concerns before the Lord. The struggle will often be between our will and God's will. The temptation to quit and avoid pain and suffering will always be there. For those who are able to struggle with God in prayer and to overcome the temptation to quit or opt for an easier road, Gethsemane would have raised their spiritual stature and made them persons after God's own heart.

Fourthly, Radical leaders also understand the Damascus Road (Acts 9)

These are moments when God will meet with us in unexpected situations and re-direct us along a fresh path of His choice. As Paul was redirected from persecuting Christians to becoming an apostle for Jesus, God can do the same in our lives. There will be these encounters and God will direct us into a ministry of mission of His choosing.

Radical leaders accept the price of leadership because they know of the glorious prize

Radical leaders know of the victor's prize. If you read Revelation 2: 7,11,17, 26; 3:5, 12, you will note that these passages talk about the "conqueror" and his prize. There is always a reward for the conqueror. In other words, they know of the banqueting table that Christ has prepared; they know of the house of many mansions; they know of the victors' wreath, they know of the blessings received as they share their lives in service. There will be a glorious prize for those who are willing to pay the price of leadership.

Developing radical leadership

The question we ask is, 'How do we develop radical leadership?'

I have spent many years developing and mentoring leaders. In the last five, I set aside time to mentor three groups of leaders. The first group is a group of six newly appointed pastors-in-charge of churches. I spend once a month meeting with them, mentoring them and listening to their challenges, issues and dreams. The group serves also as a kind of support group, encouraging each other. From time to time, I bring these pastors with me on a mission or preaching assignment. In this way they can watch me handle situations and learn by observing. In other words, I model the way.

The second group consists of probationary ministers. These are what we call "members on trial". I meet with them once a month. I listen to them as they share their challenges and go through with them areas of concern that are highlighted at each session. The goal is to help them succeed in their preparation for ordination.

The third group of leaders are young laypersons that I meet once a year at a Conference called "the Conference of Young Methodist Leaders". These are handpicked laypersons selected from the various Methodist Churches by their pastors, and funded by their respective churches to attend this three-day Conference. We challenge our young leaders to dream dreams through "intentional mentoring".

We have a large pool of young leaders who come to the Young Leaders Conference every year and each year the numbers attending increase. Since the first Conference five years ago, some of these young leaders have taken positions of leadership in their church boards and some have responded to God's call to fulltime service.

Conclusion

I would like to conclude with a poem as a challenge. The poem is found in J Oswald Sanders' book 'Spiritual Leadership' and written by George Liddell (1967, p.15). It says

Give me a man of God – one man,
Whose faith is master of his mind,
And I will right all wrongs
And bless the name of all mankind

Give me a man of God – one man,
Whose tongue is touched with heaven's fire,
And I will flame the darkest hearts
With high resolve and clean desire

Give me a man of God – one man,
One mighty prophet of the Lord,
And I will give you peace on earth,
Bought with a prayer and not a sword.

Give me a man of God – one man,
True to the vision that he sees,
And I will build your broken shrines
And bring the nations to their knees.

God is saying to you 'give me a man (when I say a man, it includes a woman). God is looking for that one person who will submit himself or herself to Him. You will be surprised as to what God can do with that one person. Are you that man? Are you that woman? What is your response?

Visionary Leadership
Rev Wes Griffin

Wes Griffin is the founder of the International Leadership Institute, training leaders of leaders for the goal of world evangelization. He has been a Methodist pastor in the USA and spent a time as a missionary in Estonia, where he helped establish a Bible College. He has a global vision.

> A **blind** person's world is bounded by the limits of his or her **touch**;
> An **ignorant** person's world by the limit's of his or her **knowledge**;
> A **great** person's by the limits of his or her **vision**.
>
> - E. Paul Hovey

Liverpool – Saturday, May 25, 1861. The Annual Convention of the Methodist New Connexion listened intently as a new proposal was presented. The request was straightforward. Rev. William Booth felt called by God to be an evangelist. The discussion became a debate, so the convention moved to a closed session of voting members only. William Booth's request was denied and he was reassigned as a circuit minister.

In the weeks that followed, Booth's heart and mind continued to confirm that God was calling him to be an evangelist. Prayerfully, on July 18, 1861, Booth wrote the Reverend H. O. Crofts, D.D., President of the Methodist New Connexion, his resignation letter:

> "You ask me to tell you frankly what I intend to do . . . I once again say that I intend to be an evangelist . . . if after a fair trail (period), I fail in reaching that sphere, I will give it up and conclude that I have been mistaken, but not until then. . . Therefore, intensely painful though it may be, I place my resignation in your hands . . .

> I do this after painful deliberation. I know what I am sacrificing, and I know I am exposing myself and those whom I love to loss and difficulty. But I am impelled to it by a sense of duty to souls, to the Church, and to God. Were I to waver, and give up for fear of the difficulties which just now appear to block my path, I feel sure that I should in the future reproach myself with cowardice in the case of my Master, and that even those who differ with me in opinion would say that I was not true to the professions I made in the Conference, when I said I had offered myself to the Lord for his work if I went forth, "without a friend and without a farthing."
>
> Trusting in God alone, I offer myself for evangelistic work."

With those words, William Booth acted on the vision that God placed in his heart. He stepped into a future that only God could see clearly. His actions were not blind faith. They were rooted in what he saw as the needs of people, the current state of the church, and in God's passion to reach people with the life transforming power of the Gospel.

Commenting on the church, he said, "I was satisfied that the methods of the average local congregation were out of date. They had ceased to attract the people to the Church – at any rate, in the city – I was not satisfied with the chapel itself, with its grey dull walls, detached life, class pews, and high-toned preaching. I was even dissatisfied with my own work."

Affirming Booth's vision, the Rev. Mr. Shone, a man converted under William's earlier ministry, invited both William and Catherine for seven weeks of services starting on August 11. Seven weeks became eighteen months as God opened the heavens and sent "an awakening" unparalleled since John Wesley's day. Fisherman rowed ten miles. Villagers would walk miles. Businessmen reported a drop in commerce during revival services. More than seven thousand Cornish men and women found peace with God. Everywhere William and Catherine turned they found a hunger for

God. They were walking in the vision that God had given them. More invitations came.

William and Catherine experienced countless challenges and obstacles. Yet, as the vision unfolded, God confirmed that they were to reach beyond the walls of the church and go "downward to the masses." During a weeklong meeting in East London at a place called Mile End Waste, William saw once again the scourge of poverty and lost souls among the starving, sick, and dying. His heart broke for a city with three million people and 100,000 paupers.

Returning home, he gazed into Catherine's eyes and said, "Darling, I've found my destiny. It's a human jungle out there. I've been walking in the midst of it. It is as bad as any tiger-infested jungle in darkest Africa."

William Booth unmistakably knew God's vision for his life. He had found his jungle. The vision clarified even further. He would go to the masses. He would live out the edict: The salvation of the soul is the key to the salvation of the body. He would go to his jungle. He would preach the Gospel. He would minister to practical, human need. Today, the world's largest relief agency, The Salvation Army with over one million "soldiers," owes its legacy to a visionary leader who was willing to see with God's eyes and walk into a future that only God could know.

What is God looking for today?

God is looking for visionary leaders who will bring the Kingdom of God to earth. This woman or man will seek God's vision for their lives until it is found. This person will be an instrument of revival and renewal. He or she will be a change agent and stand among those biblically committed servants who receive God's vision, set goals, mobilize the Body of Christ, and overcome obstacles in order to accomplish God's vision.

Nothing has changed in God's heart. The passion of Christ remains the same. God desires that the Kingdom of heaven comes on earth and that every person experience the life transforming power of the Gospel. Sadly however, the absence of the Kingdom of God is evident, and two-thirds of the world has yet to respond to the Gospel.

Who in this generation will rise up to be visionary leaders? Who in this generation will see the way God sees, feel the way God feels, hear what God hears, and will lead God's people to bring the Kingdom of God on earth?

Leadership begins with vision

All effective leadership begins with vision: a clear mental picture that inspires passion and action. Vision clarifies purpose, establishes priorities, sets standards of excellence, motivates commitment, and maximizes potential. Vision reaches out to the future.

Defining vision for ministry, George Barna states:

> 'Vision for ministry is a clear mental image of a preferable future imparted by God to chosen servants and is based on an accurate understanding of God, self and circumstances.'

God's normal means to bring the Kingdom of God on earth is to find a person and give them a vision by the power of the Holy Spirit. The vision allows a person to see that which is not yet here. It captures the heart, mind, and emotions. With vision, a leader feels God's heartbeat. With vision, a person sees the future that God desires and moves in that direction.

Vision is like the eye of an eagle. You see farther than others see. Vision is like a magnifying glass. You see more clearly than others see. Vision is like the banks of a river. Vision provides direction and purpose. Proven leaders demonstrate contagious, compelling vision. Vision leads to motivation, which leads to action, which leads to your destiny. Vision is so powerful that if you tell me your vision, then I can predict your future.

Finding God's vision for your life

The challenge is to find God's true vision for your life. Just yesterday, I spoke with a friend who knows that he is not living God's vision for his life. He has a good job with a respectable organization, yet he feels stagnant and his passion is slowly drying up. He is becoming cynical. Inside, he is dying by degrees.

Too often, we think that vision is related to some mystical experience such as a Spirit-inspired dream at night, or hearing the voice of God or an angel. However, these are not the normal means by which God gives vision to a person. God's normal tool is to open the eyes and heart of a leader to see a human need, to feel that need deeply, and to realize that God is calling the person to meet that need. To illustrate this process, let's consider Nehemiah, one of God's great visionary leaders.

Nehemiah – A true visionary leader

After the death of Solomon, God judges the nation of Israel through the Babylonian captivity. The walls of Jerusalem are broken down. The gates burned. The national treasures are stolen. The Jewish people are captured and forcibly marched fourteen hundred kilometres to Babylon. Nothing changes for 150 years. Generations live in captivity with their homeland in ruins. Eventually, a remnant returns to Jerusalem, yet nothing changes until the unlikely Nehemiah accepts God's vision. One person, with vision, becomes God's chosen instrument to rewrite history by rebuilding the walls in just fifty-two days. Let's look at how God birthed vision in Nehemiah's life.

Opening the eyes of your heart

Nehemiah was the cupbearer to the king. He had no authority over his life. He had no financial resources. He was a servant before the king. Yet, God opened the eyes of his heart to see a great need in Jerusalem, a city that he had never seen except in his imagination. A remnant had tried to rebuild the city walls, but opposition leaders convinced the king that rebellion was in the air. So, the king ordered the destruction of the walls once again. Because of his insider knowledge within the palace, Nehemiah knew of the king's order, yet he was hoping the opposition would be thwarted. However, when Hanani, his brother, returned from a visit to Jerusalem, he reported the news that "the remnant there in the province who survived the captivity are in great distress and reproach, and the wall of Jerusalem is broken down and its gates burned with fire."

The eyes of Nehemiah's heart see the destruction. He sees the rubble. He smells the charred city gates. He feels the people living in fear and insecurity. His soul experiences the oppression. Though he had never been to Jerusalem, he sees it. God is beginning the seeding process in the birth of vision. Nehemiah sees the need. The eyes of his heart are opened.

Feeling the need deeply

Everyone sees needs. They are all around us. Yet, when God is birthing vision, then a person not only sees the need, but he or she feels the need deeply. Nehemiah wept when he heard the Jerusalem report. His heart broke. His soul felt pain. The tears could not be contained.

The natural human reaction to pain is avoidance. Yet for God to birth vision, a person must be willing to enter into the pain of the need. You must be willing to identify such that your emotions are engaged as your mind embraces the facts. Whenever you encounter a person of vision, you find a person who is willing to identify himself or herself fully with the need. They are willing to feel the need deeply.

Nehemiah mourned over Jerusalem. He fasted and prayed. A vision was taking root in his heart. Awareness grew to concern and concern to a burden. The situation in Jerusalem became unacceptable. Something must be done. Burdens increase passion. Burdens birth great vision.

In January, we were in Kenya for a national training conference with the organization we serve, the International Leadership Institute. Thirty leaders spent one week hungering to be more effective in leadership, evangelism, and multiplication. One evening the Holy Spirit fell upon the group during a closing prayer session. I noticed one man, Stephen, weeping profusely as he prayed.

The next day, I asked him, "Stephen, last night something was happening in you as you prayed. What was happening?" Stephen replied, "God has given me a vision and a burden for street children who are Aids orphans. The work is very difficult. Last night God spoke again in my heart and reconfirmed the vision. I carry a great burden for these children. Thirty of them now call me "daddy." The tears you saw were tears of joy as God whispered in my ear that I am living my life purpose."

I asked about his children. Stephen's eyes twinkled as he shared. Finally, I asked, "How is it that you feel so deeply about these children?" Stephen responded, "I don't often tell people, but I was once one of them. I was living on the streets. God took me off the streets, saved me, and gave me a home. Now, I know the pain that these children are going through. I know the burdens that they carry having lost their parents to AIDS. I know what it is like to search through garbage to try and find food to eat. And, I know that I am called to bear the burden and know the blessing of helping to change their lives."

A person must be willing to embrace both the burden and the blessing of the vision. Your heart will be pulled toward the need as the vision grows. At the same time, due to the difficulties or pain or challenges your heart and mind will be tempted to withdraw. Nehemiah knew that he was a mere servant in the king's palace, yet he knew something must be done. I imagine that he spent considerable time thinking about many people who were more qualified, more talented, and more available. Yet, the Holy Spirit kept the need before Him until Nehemiah began to realize God was calling him to meet the need.

Taking the first step

Nehemiah knew it was time to step over the line and walk into the vision. For five months, he had prayed. Now he must take action. As Bruce Wilkinson states, "if this is a true vision struggling to be born, then you will develop an internal accountability for the need. You feel a sense of responsibility and urgency to do something. Softly wrapped around the burden is the quiet persistent confidence that you are being called by God to take action."

Courage and faith are required to take this step of obedience. By taking it, you acknowledge the power of God. You validate your accountability to God and to people. It may only be a small act on your part, but when you take it, there is no turning back.

On January 27, 1985 I travelled all day in a snowstorm with an engagement ring in my pocket. Arriving at Joy's dormitory late at night, we walked to the campus chapel where under stained glass lighting I asked her to marry me. After she said "yes," I said, "Let's go call our parents!" Our eyes fixed, and for an instant, we could read each other's minds, "Right now, only the two of us know about this decision. If we tell others, there might be no backing up!" It was a fleeting moment and we have laughed about it often. We did step over the line and called our parents. Soon, it seemed the whole world knew of our engagement.

For Nehemiah, a moment came when the king looked at him and said, "Nehemiah, why is your face sad though you are not sick? This is nothing but sadness of heart." Fears, doubts, and questions all raced at once through Nehemiah. He was never to bring his personal sadness before the king. What would happen if he answered truthfully? Taking a deep breath and saying a short prayer, Nehemiah responded, "If it please the king, Jerusalem lies in ruins, send me to rebuild it."

Taking the initial step and launching the vision requires faith and risk. It moves a person from the private to the public arena. You realize that you are the person God is calling and now is the time. This is God's purpose for your life. God's vision resides within. You walk into the vision. You are now a person of destiny and history will never be the same.

Dreaming God's dream

By 1992, Joy and I had served eight years in pastoral ministry. Our next big plan was to plant a church in the sprawling suburbs of a major city to reach the unchurched. At the same time Asbury Seminary offered us a full scholarship for doctoral studies in leadership and preaching as preparation. Within a few weeks of arriving on campus, I had a clear sense however that God was going to open another door.

One October afternoon, the great missionary and leader J.T. Seamands served as a guest lecturer. The Holy Spirit took Dr. Seamand's words and began speaking deeply to my heart. There were no audible voices or mystical experience, but there was a deep, unmistakable inner awareness. Dr. Seamands explained that there are times when God opens doors. He continued, "These doors do not stay open forever, and every opportunity must be taken." He shared illustrations from history, particularly India in the early 1900's.

As Dr. Seamands spoke, the Holy Spirit also spoke in my heart saying, "Fifteen months ago, I, the Lord, moved my finger and took down the iron curtain of the Soviet Union. Three hundred million people in eleven time zones can now hear the Gospel without restriction. Will you go to the frontlines?" When the class ended, I left the building, looked up into a crystal clear blue sky, and said, "Yes Lord." God was calling us out of our comfort zone.

Step by step the vision unfolded. Doors opened and doors closed. We moved to Tallinn, Estonia, one of the former soviet republics in the Baltic States. We then had the privilege to be on the team that planted the Baltic Methodist Theological Seminary. We were on the frontlines of training leaders for a part of the world that had been closed to the Gospel for more than fifty years.

Vision will take you places you never planned to go and vision will take you there faster than you ever imagine. The seminary was to begin with fifteen students and four faculty members. God's plans were much bigger. With only six months of preparation, the seminary opened with fifty-two students and nine faculty members. The school operated in three languages: Estonian, Russian, and English. I was privileged to be the founding Dean. Joy and I served on the founding faculty. Each year the enrolment increased, and today, this leadership-training ministry is one of the largest seminaries in Europe by enrolment with nearly two hundred students.

We experienced miracle after miracle as we equipped leaders for the Baltic States and Russia. These leaders knew their language and culture. They were passionately committed to reaching their regions with the Gospel. They were sacrificial in the service for Christ. There were many challenges but the constant miracles and the great sense of satisfaction confirmed that we were in the centre of God's will. We also did not know that our lives were about to be turned upside down.

Overcoming obstacles

The doctor pulled back the curtain of the examination room. One look at his face and I knew it was not good news. "You have cancer. It is in two places. You need to leave my office and go straight to see a surgeon. Your situation is urgent. You can seek a second opinion if you desire, but it is not necessary. Action must be taken quickly." Suddenly, we were no longer on the mountain top.

We had returned to the U.S.A for a period of time. I knew that something was not right in my body. We expected to hear, "Take this medicine and you will be fine in a week." Instead, major surgery was scheduled followed by three months of radiation and chemotherapy, followed by another six months of chemotherapy.

We went from living our dreams to battling for survival. The Body of Christ wrapped their arms of love around us. Joy and I, along with our two children, Hannah and Caleb, drew close to one another. For months, I only had the strength to get out of bed, go to the hospital for treatment, and return to the bed. Joy was my constant source of encouragement and strength. The only thought on our mind was survival. The issue of God's vision for our life was a distant memory. Five months into the battle, in the course of four days, three friends contacted us. They had not spoken to one another, yet all three said the exact same words, "If God gives you a vision, I want to help you achieve it."

With those words, the Holy Spirit blew on an ember deep within my soul. A small flame jumped to life. I began to realize that this was not a "sickness unto death." We began to seek God for the future. Physically, I barely had the strength to get out of bed for short periods of time, but in my spirit, God was raising up a vision. At Christmas that year, I read on a calendar a statement by Corrie ten Boom, "Every person God puts in your life, every experience you have, is the perfect preparation for the future that only God can see."

The Holy Spirit reminded us that for seven years we had been equipping leaders for the frontlines of renewal and revival on an international level. With cancer, I thought that vision had died, but now the Holy Spirit was blowing fresh wind. Still on chemotherapy, we talked with key leaders around the world. We all heard two voices, the voice of those who do not yet know Christ, and the voice of leaders who are saying equip me and I will reach my nation with the Gospel. Three weeks after the last chemotherapy session, God birthed the International Leadership Institute (ILI) to train and mobilize leaders of leaders around the world to reach their nations with the Gospel. In 2004, more than 3000 leaders around the world received advanced training in leadership, evangelism and multiplication. Each year the number of leaders who will receive ILI training is projected to increase.

The power of vision

The great need of today is men and women of vision. God is looking for those individuals who are willing to see what God sees, feel what God feels, hear what God hears, and go where God calls. God gives vision to chosen men and women to bring the Kingdom on earth. With vision, you will go to places you never intended to go. You will encounter obstacles that you never wanted to face. And, you will know the power and presence of God in your life. You will know that you are a person of purpose. You will know that you are making a difference. You will know the power of vision.

A man was fishing just offshore in a small boat. Another man was onshore watching. Every time the fisherman caught a large fish, he threw it back into the lake. Every time he caught a small fish, he kept it. The observer was confused. Finally, the observer called out, "Sir, tell me why do you keep the small fish and throw the large fish back?" The fisherman reached down into the bottom of the boat and lifted up a small cooking skillet. He shouted back, "I only have a small pan."

Don't live your life with a small vision. Don't settle for small fish. The needs of the world are too great. Dream God's dreams. Live the vision for which you were created. Set goals to keep you moving forward. Motivate others to join you in the vision. Overcome the obstacles by the power of the Holy Spirit. Change history. And never forget the words of Jesus, "I am with you always."

'Looking over your shoulder'
Rev Graham Horsley

Graham Horsley is the Methodist Connexion officer responsible for Evangelism and Church Planting. Previously he was minister of a growing cell-based church in Oldham, Manchester. He has been an encouraging influence in the emergence of fresh expressions of church in Methodism.

If you want to know whether you're a leader – look over your shoulder!

This may be a trite way of describing leadership, but it holds an important truth. Leaders are not appointed by the church, they are created by God to be leaders and anointed by the Holy Spirit to fulfil their ministry. A leader cannot help but lead – it is who they are. However, not every leader fulfils his/her potential - in fact, very few do. Most leaders grow fairly rapidly when they first begin. However, most reach a plateau where they find that their ministry is bearing fruit and they have some effectiveness, but their ministry is not as fruitful as it could be. They find themselves continually confronting the same problems and crises that make them tired and ineffective. They repeat the things which have previously borne fruit, but they also repeat the mistakes that minimise the fruit. Sometimes they blame the followers for their lack of fruit rather than examining their leadership styles more closely.

How can a leader break through this plateau into a more fruitful ministry? If you've been in leadership for a number of years, how can you 'finish well'? To put it another way, how can a leader overcome the human weaknesses that prevent them from reaching their potential? How can leaders find a practical holiness which enhances their ministry and makes the very best of their unique personality?

A major problem is that our received models of leadership are unhelpful. Ministers are trained with a high level of initial input which is largely divorced from the actual work they will be doing. They then receive very little ongoing support or accountability. This is very different from a biblical model of leadership development. Biblical leadership development is much closer to a traditional apprenticeship model than a university academic one. There is little initial training, but rather an ongoing relationship of support. There is also a much more individual relationship in the original selection of a disciple and the ongoing mentoring or coaching relationship. The mixed reception that the current self-accompanied appraisal system in the British Methodist Church has received, for example, is because of the difficulty that an institutional system has in matching the individual chemistry between accompanist and minister. When it works well both have a good experience – when the relationship doesn't gel, it's hard for the institutional system to adjust.

What does biblical leadership development look like?

The first quality is that biblical leadership always seeks to empower other leaders. Paul reminds the Ephesian church that the leadership giftings of apostle, prophet, evangelist, pastor and teacher are intended *'to prepare God's people for works of service so that the body of Christ may be built up'.*[1] The sort of leadership which is protective and defensive of status and rights has nothing to do with biblical leadership. If leaders seek to empower others, there is a high degree of likelihood that they will also seek to be empowered. Christian Schwarz' research about healthy churches shows that leaders who empower others are the ones who are most likely to seek outside help for their own ministries[2] – they practise what they preach!

This may seem to be a logical assumption about leadership, but it is not always present in the Methodist Church. Too often, ministers

1 Ephesians 4:11-12

2 Natural Church Development Handbook, Christian A Schwarz, BCGA, 1996, p23

are lonely isolated individuals who do not enjoy either accountability or empowerment. This can result in them not responding well to those who come alongside to support and empower, particularly if there is a defined accountability in the relationship. Most leaders are open to having someone with whom they can talk things through, but are hesitant about a more formal relationship. This does not sit well with our Methodist roots based on intentional discipleship within a band meeting. Most Methodist circuit staff meet irregularly and function at the level of a business meeting. Some go a step further and become a fellowship. Few go far enough to encourage and support accountability.

There are a number of models around that try to rectify this situation and rediscover accountability as a means to growth in ministry and maturity:

- Mutual accountability – the modern day band meeting
- Mentoring
- Coaching
- Spiritual direction
- Accompaniment

There are areas of overlap between these approaches and sometimes they are defined differently.

Mentoring is primarily about asking the question 'how are you doing?' It's about whole person development. Coaching is about asking the question 'what are you doing?' It is more task focussed, but will still have within it elements of character formation. Spiritual direction is about developing to spiritual maturity (which will inevitably lead to enhanced performance in ministry). Whilst accompaniment is about helping people to see and understand who they are and what they are doing clearly so that they can formulate for themselves the way to develop.

All of these approaches have strengths and weaknesses and any of them is better than no outside help at all! In this chapter we propose to look in some detail at two of them: mutual accountability and coaching.

Mutual accountability

Therefore confess your sins to each other and pray for each other so that you may be healed.
James 5:16

There are a number of approaches to this available.[3] They all share common factors but have individual distinctives. Common factors include:

- Small group approach – they require a high degree of trust, honesty and openness which is difficult to maintain with a group of more than six people. They work most easily with 2-4 people.
- Many are single sex groups (honest sharing is easier).
- They meet regularly (ideally weekly) but do not require a long meeting (one hour maximum). They work well in a work environment either immediately before or after the working day or even in a lunch hour.
- They have a small number of questions which each member of the group answers in turn.
- They end with prayer (around specifics raised in the sharing)
- The next meeting will often begin by picking up threads from the week before and discussing how things have developed.

The great strength of groups like this is that they take the day to day life of the members seriously. Many church groups find it very hard to relate seriously to the work and family pressures that all of us wrestle with. This is a huge help in ongoing discipleship development. When people who work in similar jobs share in this way, there can be a real empathy about the pressures that the individuals are under and a real determination to help one another to cope well. It is a sobering thought when struggling with temptation to know that a good friend is going to be asking searching questions about that area of temptation within a few

3 City Bands, described in Loving the lost, Lawrence Singlehurst, Kingsway 2001 pp202-5; London Institute for Contemporary Christianity have also developed a format for a modern day band meeting; Life Transformation Groups information on www.coachnet.org

days! It can make the difference between succumbing and resisting!

Questions for use in a mutual accountability group

My group uses five questions (a simplified version of the Life Transformation Group material):

- How is your relationship with God?
- How is your relationship with spouse and family?
- How are you handling your money?
- How are you facing and dealing with sexual temptation?
- How are you dealing with anger?

Laurence Singlehurst suggests a simpler framework:[4]

- Presence – a time of prayer and/or Bible reading, acknowledging the presence and the power of Jesus in the midst of the group
- Pressure – each member may share in turn a pressure they are facing (particularly at work).
- Purpose – seeking God's heart for the city, their workplaces and their lives

Groups like this take a good deal of time to build up the sort of trust that makes really honest sharing possible. This process cannot be hurried. They also depend on human chemistry – some groups may have great difficulty achieving real honesty because the people involved find it difficult to really trust each other enough. They also depend on a non-judgemental approach (that doesn't mean avoiding the hard issues, it does mean doing it in an encouraging, upbuilding way).

Coaching

There are many biblical illustrations of a coaching type relation:

- Jethro & Moses
- Moses & Joshua
- Jonathon & David
- Barnabas & Paul
- Lois/Eunice & Timothy
- Priscilla/Aquila & Apollos

4 Loving the Lost, Laurence Singlehurst, Kingsway, 2001, pp202-205

- Paul & Timothy
- Jesus & the Twelve

None of them give a complete blueprint of how the coaching relationship worked, but its impact can be seen in the developing ministries of those being coached. If we look particularly at the way Jesus dealt with the twelve, we can see a number of principles that can be applied today:

- After a time of prayer, Jesus called the disciples to himself
- He shared his whole life with them, not just his public ministry
- He gave them more time than any of the others who followed after him
- He followed a rabbinic model of teaching and equipping the disciples
- He taught them using a lot of parables and questions
- One of them betrayed him

Prayer and Calling

> *One of those days Jesus went out to a mountainside to pray, and spent the night praying to God. [13] When morning came, he called his disciples to him and chose twelve of them, whom he also designated apostles:* Luke 6:12-13

This passage is the confirmation of a process that had begun earlier and it sums up beautifully how the process works. Selecting the disciples was first and foremost a matter of spiritual discernment. This is echoed in the challenge set by the apostles to the early church in Acts 6:3: *Brothers, choose seven men from among you who are known to be full of the Spirit and wisdom.* The task was a simple administrational one of distributing food fairly, but the apostles recognised that it was a leadership role and therefore required spiritual gifts not just human ones. It is so important that those of us who are leaders are spiritually refreshed so that we can carry out this task of discernment.

After prayer, Jesus called the disciples to him. Apart from his death and resurrection, this was the most significant act in Jesus earthly ministry. He influenced many people during his three years of ministry – he discipled twelve. The gospel writers do not tell us how he decided on the twelve and what exactly he was looking for as he began the selection process. However, it is clear that this was a very intentional process on Jesus' part. It's also worth noting that it was Jesus who called the disciples to himself. No doubt part of his discernment process was identifying those who were willing to be called and to be disciples. Sadly, my personal experience of ministry has very rarely involved being called by someone who is a mature leader to become a disciple. As I look at my own track record as a leader, I see that I have too often modelled what I have experienced rather than what I see in the life of Jesus – I suspect I'm not alone!

Sharing all of life

When we think of being equipped as leaders what do we expect? Often we feel we need to expand our knowledge, particularly our knowledge of the Bible; occasionally we think of developing particular skills which a leader needs – what we don't always appreciate is that being a leader is as much about developing character as gaining knowledge or skills. Whether we talk about 'holiness' in the traditional Wesleyan way or becoming 'Christ like', it cannot be done without impacting the whole of life. That is why Paul singles out the character of the leader when he is giving advice on being a bishop or overseer (1 Timothy 3:1-13; Titus 1:5-9). Christian character is caught – not taught.

Jesus helped his disciples to become like him by being willing to share his whole self with them. Some Christian leaders try to keep relationships with church members at a 'professional' level, creating distance from the people they serve. If we adopt this model of leadership, we are making it impossible for the people that we would like to help to learn from our character in its fullest sense. Jesus was happy to let his disciples share in his laughter and his sadness. He was desperate for their support in his final testing in the garden of Gethsemane – too many leaders try to hide their fears and doubts, not realising that coping well in the hard times is the best help they can give to their followers.

Most of his time

How should leaders spend their time? I'm not asking what sort of jobs a leader should do, but rather with whom should a leader spend their time? An unstated assumption in many Christian circles is that the leader should divide their time evenly with their members, with a bias towards the elderly, infirm and needy. This is not the Jesus model. He spent most of his time with his disciples – the group of leaders that he had called to himself. Beyond that there was a spectrum of people, some of whom only ever heard the parables and enjoyed the miracles, some of them were around almost as much as the disciples (it was from this group that Matthias was chosen to replace Judas (Acts 1:26)). Whilst Jesus was happy to influence the wider group, he was determined to disciple the smaller one.

The cell church movement has reminded us of the centrality of this way of working, but it is an interesting question how many Christian leaders today see their primary task as identifying, calling and equipping a small group of leaders. In the short term, this does not seem to be the most productive way of working, but in the long term, it will certainly bear the most fruit. In parts of the world where revival is happening, it is the only way of channelling what God is doing. This was the genius of 18th Century Methodism. The class meetings developed leaders in small groups. Gifts could easily be identified and released.

Rabbinic method

This is more like an apprenticeship model than a college model of training. A low level of initial training is followed by a high level of ongoing support. Increasing numbers of Methodist ministers are trained in part-time courses rather than in full time theological colleges. However, the underlying attitude does not take relational development seriously enough.

Questions and parables

Jesus' approach to teaching was to tell parables that were capable of many interpretations to get people thinking. He was then happy to let them walk away if that what their wish. Some people came back and asked questions – they were the ones who received further teaching. Even so Jesus method of offering further teaching was very much one of asking questions rather than making statements. Similarly today, the art of the coach is not in telling people what to do, but in asking the sort of questions that help them to work out their own way forward.

Judas betrayed him

However good a coach is, s/he can only help someone to make choices. There are no guarantees how that person will turn out. A coach has a certain level of responsibility for a person, beyond that the person must take responsibility for their decisions good or bad. Some coaching relationships are even more complicated – look at the relationship between Paul and John Mark in Acts and the Epistles. In Acts 13:5 he is chosen to accompany Paul & Barnabas on their first missionary journey, in Acts 13:13 he returns to Jerusalem. In Acts 15:15 Paul and Barnabas disagree violently about his suitability as a trainee apostle – Paul goes off with Silas whilst Barnabas takes Mark back to Cyprus (the scene of his desertion and failure) to rehabilitate him. Luke tells us no more of this story, but if we look at the greetings in Paul's letters, we see that Mark is to be welcomed (Colossians 4:10) and is helpful to Paul in his ministry (2Timothy 4:11). Coaches and coachees are imperfect humans and there is a lot of give and take required in their relationships.

The above barely scratches the surface of the ministry of Jesus, but it does offer some important pointers for those of us called by God to be leaders. We are all uniquely equipped by the Holy Spirit for ministry. We are all imperfect and could do better in ministry. We could all benefit from someone coming alongside to help us in our ministry. We are all required by God to empower others in ministry. The hardest part is taking time in our hectic lives to really look at our ministries and seek appropriate help.[5] As an avid reader for many years, it took me while to accept that this sort of help is best found in other people, not in the latest Christian best-seller!

5 For more information about coaching see http://www.crmnet.org.uk/

Leadership: Future View
Rev Ashley Cooper

Ashley Cooper is the Methodist Co-ordinator of District Evangelism Enablers. He also works part time in the Cheshire district as Evangelism Enabler and has helped set up a café church in his local town. Ashley spear-headed the first UK Methodist Call to Prayer event in 2004. He is looking to stimulate mission-minded leaders.

'Jesus called them together and said, "You know that those who are regarded as rulers of the Gentiles lord it over them, and their high officials exercise authority over them. Not so with you. Instead, whoever wants to become great among you must be your servant and whoever wants to be first must be slave of all"' (Mark 10 vs. 42-44).

'Leadership is the articulation of a vision and the inspiring of others to share that vision. Leaders need to concentrate on the big picture, to think strategically and, therefore, they have to delegate the detail to others. Leadership is not about giving orders, but bringing others along. Through their vision and interaction with others, effective leaders create conditions in which people want to follow. Even very hierarchical organisations, such as the armed forces, understand the need for leaders to be respected and trusted.' (Quotation from the Methodist Church Report 2002 'Leadership in the Methodist Church')

'There is a lack of strong leadership' is a common cry from the congregation.
What do we mean by 'strong leadership'?
Who do we want to give us leadership?

What does leadership look like in the emerging church, the church that is coming to birth?

The key problem is that most of our mainstream churches have given little time and emphasis to training leaders from within their Christian community, they have assumed that the leaders will be brought in – sent to them. The result of this has been to disempower the local congregations to the extent that many of them are now totally reliant on the brought-in pastor to do everything. This is certainly a far cry from the Jesus model of leadership. Let's start by briefly looking at how Jesus developed leaders. The gospels show us he invested the majority of his time in a small number of people. He spent his life with the 12, taking time out to be with them explaining his strategy and mission. He was also fully aware, from the start that the future of the work would rest with them.

He followed a very simple model of leadership: -
Receiving vision:- He had the vision, through spending time with his father.
Communicating vision:- He communicated that vision through spending time with the twelve, teaching and training at every stage, even before they had fully grasped all the ins and outs of the mission.
Releasing vision:- He released the vision and equipped the future leaders in the emerging church.

So let us take that simple model and apply it particularly to the emerging church context.

Receiving vision – there is no substitute for spending time with God. There is no shortcut to receiving vision other than spending time with the one from whom the vision comes. A leader needs to be someone whose spirituality is evident, whose relationship and walk with God is visible to the people he serves. If that relationship is seen, then the vision will be heard with credibility.

> 'Vision is at the very core of leadership. Take vision away from a leader and you cut his or her heart out. Vision is the fuel that leaders run on. It's the energy that creates action. It's the fire that ignites the passion of followers. It's the clear call that sustains

> focussed effort year after year, decade after decade, as people offer consistent and sacrificial service to God.' [1]

Where there is no vision the people perish or where there is no vision the church crumbles...eventually. In other words, you can go on for so long leading a church on a cult of personality but eventually that is seen through, as there is no real vision, direction and purpose.

What are we striving for? What are we working towards in our churches? What is the vision of our future?

If the leader does not have a clear vision, a clear picture of where he is headed, he can still lead people but they may well end up wandering around following the latest fad or fashion that comes along in the Christian world – then they end up wondering why it hasn't worked in their church or community. It was someone else's vision – it **was** a vision but **not theirs**.

The leader has the responsibility of seeking the fresh vision from God for their community– what we are seeing currently in the way things are shaping up is that there is not one vision, not one model of church, but leaders receiving radical and different visions of what their communities should and will look like. God is giving new, fresh and dynamic visions to those leaders who will seek him.

> 'Vision by its very nature is always located in the future. Those who are leaders will live in imaginative relationship with vision. They will see the future clearly; they will be able to articulate it. They can describe what it would look like and possibly even feel like when the future vision becomes present reality.'[2]

Sticking with the vision - we need a breed of leaders who are persistent. Some leaders have to carry a vision for decades before they see the vision become reality - but for all that time they carry and work towards the fulfilment of the vision. They never give up; they never assume they have got the vision wrong; they never ask

---

1 Hybels, Courageous Leadership (Zondervan 2002) p 31
2 Robinson & Smith, Invading Secular Space (Monarch) p 151

God for a new and easier vision. They simply carry it until the right moment. 'In most cases, if the Spirit of God has been the originator of the vision, then persistence will be necessary.'[3]

We remind ourselves of the story of Joshua (Numbers 13 & 14) who, with Caleb and others, was sent to explore the land of Canaan in preparation for the invasion. When they returned all the spies agreed that indeed the land was flowing with milk and honey; it was a fantastic place but it was full of giants 'we seemed like grasshoppers in our own eyes, and we looked the same to them' (Numbers 13 vs. 33) - people who were stronger than they were and all, except Joshua and Caleb, said they could go no further.

Now Joshua and Caleb had caught the vision, had grasped what God intended and although it seemed an impossible task, they grabbed on to the vision with both hands and said "Let's go – if God is for us". But the people rebelled, they didn't grasp it, they hadn't got it and they wouldn't go. So, for forty years they wandered – living in a wilderness. But Joshua held onto the vision. Joshua could see what was going to be one day and all his energy all his hope was in that. Then, at just the right time, Joshua says, "This is it, this is the moment" and they take the land. Now that's obviously a shortened version; but he was called to hold a vision for forty years before he began to see any of it comes to life.

If it is God's vision – if it has come from him – he will bring it to completion however impossible it seems to you, he will make all the resources available to you but he requires you to be persistent, to hold it, to keep pressing forward.

Communicating vision – communicating the vision is probably the most important responsibility leaders of the emerging church have. Leaders don't just have the responsibility of leading the people, they have to know to where they are leading them and the people have to know to where they are being led. This is not the blind leading the blind. It is the vision receiver sharing the vision so that all see the purpose of the journey.

---

3 Ibid p 154

If our people don't know where they are heading – where the community is being led, in other words, what the vision is – they will not buy into it with their time, talents or resources. They will not be enthusiastic for it. We have churches full of people who have not got a clear vision for their church and, therefore, there is no passion within the community – they become stagnant and change is not seen as necessary because there is no clear direction or purpose. The blame for some of the stagnation of our church must be laid mainly at the feet of the leader who either has not sought God for vision OR has not communicated the vision with the people. What happens is we either lose the people or we have a congregation that has no passion or purpose - a 'lukewarm church' (Rev 3), which God detests.

So many of our churches are just going through the motions of a previous vision – the vision of a previous generation, a vision that was received through prayer and fasting, a vision that was received through time in the presence of God by courageous leaders and communicated well – so much so that it changes a generation - but is no longer the vision that God is trying to give for today. We need leaders who will find the new vision and communicate it with the people so they can catch it, grasp it and buy into it. That is the only way we will see any form of renewal in what are seemingly 'lukewarm' or dying churches. It is the leader's responsibility.

> 'Jesus, just before he ascended into heaven, said, according to my translation of Mathew 28:19-20, "Okay team, here's the goal: Go into all the world and preach the gospel. Lead every man, woman, and child to faith. Then grow them up by teaching them to observe all I have commanded you. Ready. Set. Go." And they did.' [4]

Jesus sent them with the clearest vision possible. They knew what the task was; they bought into the received vision and gave everything for it.

> 'After Pentecost, Peter functioned as the leader of the disciples and was the principle agent of God's work of

4 Hybels, Courageous Leadership (Zondervan 2002) p 91

> reconstructing his people from the ruins of the Jewish nation. The new Christian community founded in Jerusalem after Pentecost bore all the marks of that established by Jesus among his twelve disciples. Jesus the apostolic builder had provided the basic structures for the newly emerging church.' [5]

Jesus had communicated the vision effectively so that when he was no longer there the others could carry on the work. They knew the strategy, they were equipped for the task and knew where they were heading. The emerging church, the church God is calling us into, needs leaders who not only have vision but can communicate that vision so that it is caught by all those around them, a vision that becomes a shared vision.

Releasing vision – 'Jesus went up on a mountainside and called to him those he wanted, and they came to him. He appointed twelve – designating them apostles – that they might be with him and that he might send them out to preach and to have authority to drive out demons' (Mark 3 vs. 13-15). Jesus' intention was to call the disciples to him that he might send them out – their mission was to continue the task of building the kingdom.

Michael Moynagh, in his book 'emergingchurch.intro'[6] coins the phrase 'permission giving' - 'my job is simply to bless innovations on the ground'. This is the view being expressed by some leaders in the emerging Christian communities. Once the vision of the would-be church is given with clarity, then the outworking of that needs to be released to those who catch it. 'Dynamic leadership does not think first of how to retain control but of how to give away as much as possible.' Jesus spent more time building a team of leaders, people with a passion and clear purpose than he did out on mission. Twelve people catching the vision, equipped to work the vision out would produce more fruit than one man ever could.

Yet we have churches and leaders who receive a vision but never communicate for fear of losing power, never release it out of an

---

5 Breen, the Apostle's Notebook (Kingsway 2002) p 127
6 Moynagh, emergingchurch.intro (Monarch 2004) introduction.

insecurity that means they have to remain in control of everything. A leadership that feeds them and their power and their ego rather than feeds the vision or builds new leaders. Just think how much more we would impact our communities, just dream about how many more lives would be brought into a relationship with Jesus Christ if only church leaders would take seriously the task of developing visionary leaders and releasing them out blessed by the local church. If only we were more intentional about the task of developing, vision casting, and releasing of leaders.

> 'The outcome of leadership is always the same: Christ's people are empowered. They are empowered to practise their priesthood and live in intimacy with the heavenly Father. They are empowered to live the uniqueness of their personal grace testimonies in all the relationships that God is bringing their way. They are empowered to use their Spirit gifts in all of those same relationships, as well as ministries that the Lord Jesus opens up for them.'[7]

Conclusion - a journey to the edge

Christ's call to his leaders is 'Come with me on a journey' and it is a journey that will take the church and us to the edge and into the unknown. A journey to a place where Jesus wants to do something new, pioneer a new work, plant new Christian communities. As leaders we go, but not into un-chartered territory because we know that the way has been prepared if we are following his footsteps.

> 'As God strips away the self-reliance of the mainstream denominations and takes us into the desert of dependency on Him, we will – like Moses – find ourselves being led to the mountain of meeting where God will cause his fire to fall, fire that frees us so that in turn we become the liberators that God needs to meet this hour.'[8]

We may say that the world in which we live is captive but if we look closely enough the church is just as enslaved to a past vision and

7 Robinson & Smith, Invading Secular Space (Monarch) pg 144

8 Breen, the Apostle's Notebook (Kingsway 2002) Pg 208

needs leaders who will enable it to be free to become the new thing God has in store for us.

George VI shared these words in his 1939 Christmas broadcast:

> *"A new year is at hand.*
> *We cannot tell what it will bring.*
> *If it brings peace, how thankful we shall all be.*
> *If it brings us continued struggle, we shall remain undaunted.*
> *In the meantime, I feel that we may all find encouragement in the lines, which in my closing words I would like to say to you all:*
> *'I said to the man who stood at the gate of the year, "Give me a light that I may tread safely in the unknown." And he replied, "Go out into the darkness and put your hand into the hand of God. That shall be to you better than light and safer than a known way."*
>
> *(From a poem called 'God knows' written by Miss Minnie Louise Haskins)*

What a call to leaders embarking on a journey into the emerging church!

SECTION 4: ENABLING EVANGELISTIC COMMUNITIES

Introduction
William Porter

Evangelism was the dirty 'E' word in many church circles 30 years ago; it is now the *desperate* 'E' word in the opening decade of the 21st century. Denominational heads have never been more open to the need for evangelism to be high on the agenda at strategic meetings. There has probably not been a more opportune time in which to garner the whole church into fulfilling the priority of making new disciples of Christ. But what seems to come out of our desperation, maybe something that God is using to fulfil His intention – to send us out afresh into His world and make disciples of all nations. Maybe the challenge here is to turn the church outwards with God's amazing grace.

Australian mission writers Frost and Hirsch, who are doing a lot of important thinking about post-Christian society, have put churches into two categories. They say that the church is either attractional or it is incarnational. If it's attractional we're effectively saying, 'come through our doors. We want to welcome you, bless you and help you become one of us'. But an attractional model of mission only works for those parts of the population who are used to coming inside the doors of the church. For those who are wary of religion, for many un-churched and de-churched people who don't want to darken the doors of a foreign institution, attractional church doesn't work anymore.

Frost and Hirsch highlight that we need to try another model of mission which Jesus embodied – an incarnational one. Incarnation is about being amongst people, turning ourselves inside out, becoming vulnerable as we engage people where they're at. It's saying 'we're coming to sit with you. We want to understand you, bless you and share God's life together.' It is to be like Jesus and walk amongst our community. Summarising this change of mindset, Frost and Hirsch write:

> 'the missional-incarnational church adopts a stance totally different from the attractional one. Rather than investing time in the creation and development of sacred religious spaces for people to meet God, this mode recognizes that church is a much more organic, dynamic, and non-institutionalized set of relationships than the old Christendom mode allows for. If the attractional mode sees the world as divided into two zones, the "in" and the "out," the incarnational model sees it more as a web, a series of intersecting lines symbolizing the networks of relationships, friendships and acquaintances of which church members are a part.'[1]

That is a wonderful model, but I think it only goes halfway. Why? Because I know that many churches, can be amongst people, and still have nothing to say. We can be incarnational amongst people but have no power to demonstrate the reality of God's kingdom. What Jesus, in fact, demonstrated was that he was incarnational and he was also *anointed* by God's Spirit. In Luke 4 we see a wonderful story of Jesus in Nazareth, where Jesus, anointed by the Spirit, returns in the power of the Spirit to his home town, the place where he was most earthed and incarnate – the humble carpenter's son. And the very manifesto he takes upon himself publicly is that 'the Spirit of the sovereign Lord is upon me, *the one who has grown up here* (italics mine), because he has anointed me to preach good news to the poor' (Lk 4v18).

Clark Pinnock, evangelical theologian, writes about this dimension of the church's spirituality:

> 'the church is an extension not so much of the incarnation as of the anointing of Jesus. Jesus is the prototype of the church, which now receives its own baptism in the Spirit...There had to be, after Jesus'

---

1 Frost, Michael & Hirsch, Alan, The Shape of Things to Come: innovation and mission for the 21st century church (Peabody, Massachusetts: Hendrickson Publishers, 2003) pp43-44.

> departure, a colony of heaven, living the life and power and experiencing the freedom of the kingdom.[2]'

In this understanding therefore , incarnational is not the best model of mission today, but rather *transformational*.

Incarnation + anointing = transformation.

Where God is trying to take us is, I believe, to become transformational church. In a transformational understanding we are opening our doors wide, we are turning ourselves inside out, we are focussing our energy in the community. But in doing so, we are praying that God anoints us, that we might be Jesus-led, and have Spirit-inspired impact. In fact, community transform-ation is a buzz word in some church circles.

As John Leach, Anglican renewal author, writes about revival and community transformation:

> 'Of course, revival may be (and often has been) the first step in transformation; the changes in British Society which followed the Wesleyan preaching of the gospel are well-documented, for example. But revival need not proceed to transformation, and there are examples of a move of God which has brought many into the church but left the world around relatively unscathed. It is ultimately about vision; God is so often limited in what he chooses to do by what we expect him to do, believe he can do, and cry out to him to do. So revival is a good place to begin, but it needs to go much wider than the church, and more deeply into the very fabric of society.'[3]

How does this cash out? It means that we become congregations and ministries which are having a salt and light impact – providing hope in the run down housing estates, bringing vibrant ministry in the schools, seeing a harvest amongst the marginalised; where strategic praying and partnering with police sees a decline in the

2 Pinnock, Clark, Flame of Love: a theology of the Holy Spirit (Downers Grove, Illinois: IVP, 1996) p114.

3 Leach, John, Community Transformation: a beginner's guide (Cambridge: Grove Books Ltd, 2002) p22.

crime and drug issues of our cities; where kingdom leaders are found influencing areas of business, health, law media and politics. The neighbourhoods in which we are incarnated, are being transformed as we take risking steps in anointed, Spirit inspired mission. Only God can do it. But He wants to do it through this gift called church, as we enable them to become evangelistic, transformational communities!

Growing Evangelistic Communities

Isaac Lim

I want to share some thoughts on evangelism and see how we can grow evangelistic communities in our churches. Let me begin by saying that evangelism is the single most significant indicator of a healthy church. I know this may be debatable but I believe it to be true. I believe we need to grow evangelistic communities as the church's first priority.

Why am I making this statement? I am making this statement on the basis that a healthy church is a growing church. As a healthy cell multiplies and grows, so does a healthy church.

Charis, our son, was born a very small baby slightly over three pounds in weight. When he was three months old, he was afflicted with encephalitis that almost killed him. At six years of age he was short compared to his peers. When he was in the sixth grade, his friends were about one foot taller than he. His asset however was his ability to sprint and he could outrun those much taller than he. Yet we were anxious about his growth. Eventually he did grow and we praise God for that.

One indicator of a healthy church is growth in the number of persons won for Jesus. We say we don't play the numbers game but numbers do indicate where the church is. If the great commission of Jesus Christ is to make disciples of all nations then we are in fact talking about numbers. There must be evidence of people accepting Jesus as Lord and Saviour. Hence, to me, the single most significant indicator of a healthy church is growth in the number of those accepting Jesus. Even if the growth is slow, that is alright because we grow at different rates, but at least we know that the church is growing.

Early church

When you look at the early church you will note that the early church was an evangelistic community from the very outset. When

Peter preached his first sermon on the day of Pentecost, three thousand persons were added to the church. Soon it was five thousand and so on (Acts 4:4). Then it spread to the Mediterranean region where Christian congregations were established. They were all evangelistic disciple-making communities, taking the mandate of Jesus seriously.

John Wesley

The ministry of John Wesley and the early Methodists were no different. John Wesley was an evangelist and he raised evangelistic communities. Wherever he went, he preached the message of the Kingdom of God and people received Jesus Christ. To sustain the revival, he organised new believers first into bands and later into Societies and Class Meetings. These small groups were established for the purpose of coping with the number of new believers coming to Christ through his ministry. Thousands of believers were sustained and nurtured through these means. These class meetings also functioned as evangelistic communities bringing the message of the gospel to newcomers.

Our calling

The great commission of Jesus Christ compels us to be evangelistic communities. We are to go and make disciples of all nations. The making of disciples can only take place if the gospel is first articulated. The articulation of the gospel allows the unbeliever an opportunity to accept Christ for himself and become a disciple.

In the making of a disciple, we are called to share the message of eternal life. The message of eternal life is at the very core of the gospel proclamation. The gospel message addresses issues not only of the present but also of the future and beyond. It addresses issues of heaven and hell, life, death, and the resurrection.

Many of us avoid this issue, but eternal life is the crux of our concern. We are finite beings and as there is a beginning to life, there will certainly be an end to it as well.

A few months ago when I was in the United States, I received news from my wife that a very good friend of hers had died. This was a young, vibrant, up and coming businesswoman who built an award-winning aerospace company and she was only in her mid-forties. She was being driven around in China when a huge truck rammed into her car and killed her on a Chinese highway.

Her sudden demise made me think about life. What is life all about? Whilst we want people to enjoy life while they can, they need to be prepared for life beyond the present life. In John 17 Jesus talks about eternal life and he defines eternal life as knowing '...the only true God, and Jesus Christ, whom You have sent' (John 17:3). In other words, the essence of eternal life is a personal relationship with God the Father and Jesus Christ His Son. Eternal life is an experience that begins now and continues beyond the grave. In other words eternal life is a present experience.

We dwell within the boundary of eternal life when we accept Jesus Christ as Lord and Saviour. We live in the company of God the Father, God the Son and the enabling presence of the Holy Spirit. Hence, eternal life is a present experience. It is a life that progresses from imperfection to perfection in one spiritual continuum (2 Cor.5:17; Rev 21:1-7).

As eternal life is a reality, so is eternal death. Most of us do not like to talk about eternal death. Some theologians are of the opinion that a God of love would not allow a person to be left in eternal damnation. However, it is not possible to talk about the justice of God without the judgement of God (Gal 5:19-21; Rom 3:23). The Bible says 'as it is appointed for mortals to die once, and after that the judgement' (Heb 9:27).

In Christ, there need not be any fear of death. Eternal life is the hope for all. If not, we who are Christians are of all people most to be pitied (1 Cor.15:19).

Set apart

The church is the distinct community set apart to fulfil God's mandate for a dying world. The church is given the mandate to preach the gospel, and make disciples of all nations. This is well articulated by the apostle Peter when he said, 'But you are a chosen race, a royal priesthood, a holy nation, God's own people, in order that you may proclaim the mighty acts of Him who called you out of darkness into His marvellous light. Once you were not a people, but now you are God's people, once you had not received mercy, but now you have received mercy' (1 Peter 2:9-10).

What is the call of God for us? God's call for us is to proclaim the mighty acts of Him who called us out of darkness into His marvellous light. That is why we, from the East, always think fondly of the missionaries who came to our shores many years ago to bring the message of the gospel. Now, we feel that it is our responsibility to bless the world in like manner. That is why missionaries from Singapore are found in almost every corner of the world today.

I believe that God calls us to fulfil His mandate. This is what the church alone can do because it is the church alone that has been asked to proclaim the message of eternal life. That is our unique contribution. We know the source of light and life (John 1:4). It is up to us to share the message of eternal life and let the light shine.

How we can grow evangelistic communities

We can grow evangelistic communities in various ways.

Firstly, we must act on the great commission. The work begins at our doorstep (Acts 1:8) - your loved ones, your parents, your relatives, your colleagues must be exposed to the message of the gospel. I believe that is God's call for us.

We seek the lost as Jesus sought the lost. Jesus communicated this message in the parable of the lost sheep, the lost coin and the lost son (Luke 15:4-31). If you study the three parables, you will note the intensity in the seeking of the lost, an excitement in the finding of the lost and a joyful celebration to announce the restoration of the lost. Hence, the first thing that we need to do to grow evangelistic communities is to act on the great commission.

Secondly, we need to narrow the clergy-laity divide. The laity must be drawn into the ministries of the church. Evangelism is very much the task of the laity. It is imperative that they be brought into the planning of evangelistic strategies. When we maintain the clergy/laity divide, the general expectation is for the clergy to do the evangelism while the laity waits and watches. This is not the Biblical mandate. The responsibility of the clergy is to inspire, motivate, lead and perhaps demonstrate how evangelism can be done. The main task of evangelism must be handled by the laity because they are the ones who are in direct contact with those who are yet to receive the gospel. The laity must be nurtured and empowered to do the work of evangelism.

I have in Singapore an outstanding layperson who organises evangelistic concerts every Christmas at a shopping mall. He would get church members from various Methodist churches to participate in this Christmas activity. They would present the Christmas pageant, skits, sing carols, dance, and then distribute Christmas tracts to onlookers. The whole concert is handled by lay people and some come to know Christ through this means.

Thirdly, we make evangelism the responsibility of every member and not a committee. When we have a committee on evangelism, members of the church expect the work of evangelism to be done by the committee and not by them. In Singapore we are trying to redefine the responsibility of these committees. The committee on evangelism will function as a resource group, but evangelism will be done by the whole church through the cell group network. The evangelism committee would provide the tools to do evangelism in the cell groups.

Fourthly, to grow evangelistic communities, we make evangelistic methodologies simple. When methods become too complicated no-one wants to evangelise. There are many ways of doing evangelism. I would like to suggest a simple way and that is to tell your story. Tell your friends how you came to know Jesus. Having told your story, you could invite them to consider accepting Jesus as their Lord and Saviour.

There will be times when people will come to you with their problems, their pains, and their broken dreams. Tell your story of what Jesus has done for you. You can even suggest praying for them. When the opportunity arises, you could even challenge them to accept Jesus as their Lord and Saviour.

We need to help our people share the message of the gospel simply; the simpler the method, the better. Jesus shared the message of the gospel simply. Whether it was with Zacchaeus in Jericho or the woman at the well in Samaria, Jesus made His message simple. He reached their hearts. That is why they were ready to receive His message and be transformed.

I am sure we have a story to tell of our encounter with Jesus. Begin there and be a blessing to your friends and loved ones. Of course, advance training in evangelism is always helpful but that is not crucial in telling others about Jesus. You have a story to tell about Jesus, tell it as it is.

Fifthly, if you want to raise an evangelistic community, claim a community. Decide on a community you want to win for Jesus Christ. Take a map and draw the boundary of the community you want to win for Jesus. Then decide how to do it.

A few of our churches are located in what you may call housing estates. These housing estates consist of high rise apartment blocks. Thousands of people live in these high rise apartments. Our churches would claim several of these blocks as their community for evangelism and draw the boundary within which they will serve.

Having drawn their boundary lines, they would move into these blocks through what is called "community penetration". They begin by relating to the community through child care, medical care, or simply bringing them a gift on a festive occasion. In these community events, nothing is said of the gospel. It is simply building relationships. For example, we in Singapore celebrate the Chinese Lunar New Year. Members of the church would go from house to house and distribute mandarin oranges on this occasion. They would simply say 'we are from the church and want to wish you and your family a happy and prosperous new year.' That is all that is said and they move on to the next house.

Sometimes members of the church would go to a community and clean the environment. They would clean the grounds, volunteer to wash cars, throw the rubbish and in doing so, bond with the community. Before long, the community becomes aware of the presence of the church and welcomes their presence. We then tell them about our childcare facility, our kindergarten, our young peoples' programme, or our elderly care centre. Soon they get used to coming to the church. Eventually when an invite is made for them to attend a church function like the church anniversary or a gospel film show, many of them would come to these events. Through these events, some come to know Christ as Lord and Saviour.

Of course you need to be sensitive to your own cultural context. What may work in one context may not work in another context. Hence knowing your community and what can work is important.

Finally, to grow evangelistic communities, we need to set specific goals. It is good for us to set ourselves a target as to how many persons we would like to win for Jesus. Work on a number. Let people accuse you of playing the numbers game if they wish. It does not really matter, because at the end of the day you are accountable only to God.

If we are saying that we want to win five hundred persons for Christ, what is wrong with that? You might at the end of the day only win thirty persons for Christ. Although you have not met your target, you have at least won thirty persons to Jesus. It is better to win thirty persons to Christ than none at all. Is that good? I must say it is marvellous. Of course you could do better. But at least for now, the church has grown by thirty new believers!

Jesus has commissioned us to make disciples of all nations. Let us do His bidding and hasten His coming again.

ENGAGING WITH SPIRITUAL HUNGER TODAY

Rev Dr Rob Frost

Rob Frost is director of Share Jesus International, which conducts missions and resources churches in innovative outreach. He is the founder of Easter People Christian holiday week, and a Sunday morning host of Premier Radio Show. He is a key influencer in the church today.

'Holistic' has become the buzz-word in everything from social work to education. Even the British Army has announced a more 'holistic' approach to its new recruits! But holistic medicine has grabbed most media attention.

Holistic patient care is an umbrella term for looking at the overall health and lifestyle profile of a patient. It treats specific ailments not as conditions to be alleviated but rather as symptoms of a more fundamental disease.

The first formal link between conventional and holistic medicine was established in 1989 between the Hammersmith hospital and the Bristol Cancer health centre. Conventional therapy and holistic treatment (including a vegan diet, counselling, and complete relaxation) were combined.

Many hospitals, general practitioners and health professionals now view holism as the only proper way to treat patients. They view the links between body, mind and spirit as so strong that it's impossible to treat one aspect of a human being without considering the others.

What can contemporary Christians do to respond to this growing recognition of spiritual need in society? What can the church do to demonstrate that Christ cares for the whole person? How can each of us live our lives with a more holistic view of ourselves and of those around us?

Pilgrimages

Several years ago I led a series of pilgrimages around the country. In all, more than twenty thousand people joined us on these 'prayer walks' to ancient places. It was one of the most powerful and spiritually renewing experiences of my life. I will never forget it.

Bamber Gascoigne, reviewing medieval pilgrimages, observed that a party of pilgrims set out with just as much excitement as a package tour today, and they would have been just as varied a group of people. (Bamber Gascoigne, The Christians. Cape: London, 1986).

A pilgrimage still throws together different kinds of people and breaks down the social barriers between them. Some days there were ethnic groups and middle class white suburbanites, unemployed blue-collar workers and City stockbrokers, teenagers and grandparents, and whole families, helping each other along the country trail towards their local Cathedral.

A strong sense of community develops on a pilgrimage and people support one another along the way. A pilgrim group often seems like an extended family, and if there are children present it's sometimes difficult to work out who they belong to!

A pilgrimage can be a wonderful opportunity for walking in the footsteps of the great men and women of faith of previous generations. We can learn much from them, and their devotion can spur us on to greater commitment to Christ.

One such pilgrimage begins on the Berkshire Downs and follows in the footsteps of Birinus, the missionary of Wessex. The pilgrims pause by the River Thames to remember how Birinus baptised the Saxon king which was a turning point in the life of the church. As they pause there the pilgrims thank God for the past and seek a fresh vision for the future.

Every Easter Monday hundreds of people make a pilgrimage to Canterbury Cathedral in the footsteps of Augustine, the early

Christian missionary whose monks evangelised England from AD 597.

I once joined this pilgrimage, and when we arrived at Canterbury Cathedral we all lifted up candles and passed the flame from candle to candle until they were all alight. I found it a poignant reminder that the light of Christ has been passed on down the centuries to us today.

Pilgrimages often have a prophetic role and give us a heightened awareness of the world's needs. Pilgrimage is not an escape from reality, but an opportunity to face up to the needs within us and in the world around us.

The brothers of the monastic community of Taizé in France have organised many pilgrimages around the world. These pilgrimages often have a prophetic edge to them. During their visit to London the Taizé pilgrims divided into groups to pray for the city.

I remember one group visiting an area of great racial tension. I found it deeply moving to see them praying round the area in the pouring rain. They prayed in a multiplicity of languages but they knew the unity of the Spirit. Their presence in the area was a poignant symbol of the power of Christ to unite those from different races and cultures.

Pilgrimage is ideal for families, and a good occasion for new people to come and experience Christian fellowship. I've found that the ideal pilgrim group is about twenty people, and the ideal length is about five miles.

Each group should have its own 'spiritual director'. If there are any children in the group there should be a leader designated to care for them and to develop activities along the walk which they can enjoy.

The aim of the pilgrimage is to enrich the devotional life of each participant. Simple devotional activities are devised to involve the group as they walk along toward their destination. Pilgrimage, then, is one way of encouraging all those who seek a more spiritual perspective on life. Pilgrimage should become a regular part of every church's life and ministry.

Christian Heritage

Dr. Andrew Walker is a lecturer at Kings' College in London. Several years ago he exchanged what was for him a failing form of Pentecostalism for a living spirituality based in Greek Orthodox Christianity.

He recognised his need for something richer than hymns, hand-clapping and hallelujahs and found it by connecting with the ancient prayers, disciplines and liturgies of a church which claims that it has the closest connection with early Christendom.

I empathise with his journey. I recognise that the Christian spirituality necessary to survive in society today must be far deeper than the shallow emotionalism which some of us have been getting by on.

I know that Christian spirituality will need a new depth and richness to stand alongside the diverse range of new spiritualities now on offer. If it doesn't ring true it won't relate to a spiritually focussed society.

We must delve again into the riches of our Christian heritage, and offer the world a spiritual reality which has been tried and tested over many generations. We have become shallow Christians whose spirituality bears no comparison to the depth of mysticism of earlier Christian traditions.

David Adam is the Vicar of Lindisfarne. He has written extensively about Celtic spirituality and his personal attempt to interpret their disciplines for today. He believes that we need to discover the precious links between all living things; that there is a unity at the very heart of our world, and it can be experienced by each of us. He teaches that a combination of God-awareness and ecology are basic to this approach.

In the dark ages St Aidan held out the light of Christ to a godless and secular generation. Through his influence much of England and Europe was affected by the gospel. Yet Aidan was not based in a large city or on a busy thoroughfare. His ministry was established in the obscure island of Lindisfarne, known as Holy Island, off the Northumbrian coast.

Lindisfarne is only one and a quarter miles from the shore. It's a tidal island and can only be approached when the tide is out. This gives a rhythm to its life. In recent years thousands of people have been making pilgrimage there to connect with this simple rhythm and to discover the heritage of the Celtic saints.

Aidan used to look out at a little boat at anchor to see whether the tide was coming in or going out. He built a discipline of spirituality on this daily flow of the tide. He taught his island community to receive the love of God as the tide came in, and then pour it out in intercession, praise and loving service to others as it went out. Aidan knew that too many lives become trivialized by too much action, and that each of us needs to be refreshed by the incoming tide of God's love.

Every day, between the tide coming in and the tide going out there was an hour when the tide was still. Aidan taught that when the balance between our receiving and our giving is right we, like the still waters between tides, discover perfect peace.

Gradually, more and more people visited Aidan and his praying community, including the king and the royal family. Eventually, Aidan had to create an island refuge off his island refuge in order to restore the balance between giving and receiving in his own life.

This tiny island was known as the 'desert in the ocean'. It was a place of great spiritual blessing but also a place to fight the powers of darkness both within and without. Aidan went there to be alone with God and to give priority to prayer. It was a wild rugged place and his prayers were often punctuated by the deafening roar of the sea.

Ray Simpson is the Guardian of the community of St Aidan and St Columba on Lindisfarne. He is establishing communities of Christians around the world who want to follow the spiritual disciplines of the Celtic saints. After centuries of neglect, this aspect of Christian spirituality is being rediscovered.

Busy men and women who are caught up in the pressures of a hi-tech materialistic society, are discovering that they need to connect with the ebb and flow of the tides of Lindisfarne. They have a new desire to take in from God and to give out in compassionate service. They want to discover that perfect rest which comes when the balance is right.

Thousands of Christians of all denominations visit Taizé, Iona and Holy Island to learn something of their spiritual heritage and tradition. This trend will grow even more popular in the coming decades.

If we are to make a relevant response to society's growing hunger for spirituality we must take time to connect with our Christian heritage. We must walk ancient paths, and re-learn ancient disciplines.

Spiritual mentors

Aidan recognised that it isn't easy to develop a life of prayer and contemplation so he set up a system of mentoring to encourage his followers to follow these disciplines.

Each of the brothers whom he personally mentored adopted an 'anamchara' - a cell-mate. This new member of the community would learn by rote 150 psalms, a gospel and spiritual songs which were taught him by the senior brother. In turn the younger member would take on his own 'anamchara', and so the spiritual disciplines were passed on from one to another. (David Adam. Flame in my heart. Triangle 1997).

This kind of spiritual mentoring is growing more popular again at the moment. Many committed Christians are discovering that they need a spiritual 'director' to help them in their journey of prayer and devotion.

Timothy Jones, in an article called 'Believer's Apprentice' ('Christianity Today') found that his director helped him to make sense of everyday life and to spot God's activity in the mundane. He began to get a true focus on the events of his life and gained great strength from the knowledge that his director was praying for him.

In the very helpful book 'Connecting...the mentoring relationships you need to succeed in life' by authors Stanley and Clinton (NavPress 1992) all Christians are encouraged to find a spiritual director. This director would enable believers to assess their own development in the Christian life, point out areas of strength and weakness in spirituality, and help them to take initiatives for change and growth. Above all, the spiritual director must provide accountability and give the kind of guidance which leads to spiritual maturity.

We must learn again the ancient Christian disciplines of meditation. Our goal should be to reach a life of inner stillness, and to become silent and focussed on God alone.

Perhaps many of us need to become apprentices in the spiritual life and be guided by those who are further along the journey of prayer than ourselves.

Perhaps the church needs to raise up a new generation of spiritual directors who can navigate hungry souls toward the feast of goods things which God has for us.

Meditation

I was nurtured in the evangelical school of Christian experience where the fifteen-minute 'quiet time' and regular attendance at Sunday services were advocated as the 'norm' of the spiritual life.

I sometimes think that I have been cheated, and that this kind of spirituality has shielded me from the awesome experience of meditation found in other Christian traditions.

I hope that I will soon discover something more of the richness of true Christian spirituality. I want to live in the daily reality of the Living God. I want to enter into the kind of experience which C.S. Lewis described in Letters to Malcolm:

> "In prayer this real 'I' struggles to speak, for once from this real being, and to address, for once, not the other actors, but-what shall I call Him? The Author, for He invented us all? The Producer, for He controls all? Or the Audience, for He watches, and will judge the performance? "..The prayer preceding all prayers is "May it be the real 'I' who speaks. May it be the real 'Thou' that I speak to."

It is this kind of reality which transcends the falsehood of our culture and enables us to discover God, and, in His presence to discover who we really are.

This spiritual self-discovery cannot be achieved through trendy techniques of analysis, meditation or relaxation therapy, for God must play a part in it. As C.S. Lewis concluded:

> "Only God Himself can let the bucket down to the depths in us... The most blessed result of prayer would be to rise thinking, "But I never knew before. I never dreamed..." (Letters to Malcolm. Ch 15. Fount. 1977).

Observing Christian meditation and consciousness Robert K C Forman of City University New York concludes that it is the pure consciousness event.

> "In time, with regular meditation, this stillness continues... even though lots of other things are happening around us. It becomes a permanent state. Eventually, meditation leads us to a perceived unity between ourselves and the objects around us, known as the unitive mystical state."
> ("What does mysticism have to teach us about Consciousness?" Robert K C Forman, Program in Religion, Hunter College, City University of New York. April 1996).

If the evangelists were the pacemakers of eighteenth century Christianity, the missionaries led the way in the nineteenth century, and the martyrs have been at the forefront of Christian witness in the twentieth century. Who will God raise up to lead the way in the future?

Personally, I believe that Christian mystics will be the ones with much to say to society of the over the coming years. They will model how to live in the stillness of the presence of God, and will play a significant role in shaping the society of the twenty-first century.

M. Scott Peck the eminent psychiatrist from Connecticut, is the author of the cult-best seller 'The Road Less Travelled", a book of self discovery which seems to have struck a chord with millions of people seeking inner healing and a greater sense of purpose.

Peck's book has sold well in both the USA and in Britain, and is prominently displayed in many health-food and New Age shops around the country. He became a Christian after writing that book, and explores something of the spirituality of his Christian journey in his later work 'The Different Drum.' He writes about mysticism...

> "Mysticism has a lot to do with mystery. Mystics acknowledge the enormity of the unknown, but rather than being frightened by it, they seek to penetrate ever deeper into it that they may understand more - even with the realization that the more they understand, the greater the mystery will become." (M. Scott Peck. The Different Drum, Arrow. 1990).

Disillusionment with consumerism, materialism and the mass production of our age has driven many to seek a richer 'interconnectedness', and to hunger for a new harmony with nature and the changing seasons. Essentially, this is a hunger for God.

We need to identify contemporary Christian mystics who can carry on the work of people like Teresa of Avila. She always wrote of herself in the third person and described her spiritual experience "...the essential part of her soul seemed never to move from its dwelling place." (Teresa of Avila. The Interior Castle. Trans. E Allison Peters. New York: Doubleday, 1961. p211.)

In a world of growing pressure and pain, we need to discover a form of Christian spirituality which does not separate us from the world... but which enables us to find the stillness of God's presence in the thick of the action!

Each of us must nurture that relationship with Christ which is at the heart of true Christian experience. We must give it time, and learn how to 'practise the presence of Christ'.

All of the great Christian mystics down the centuries commend this practice as the essential starting point for prayer. At the end of the seventeenth century Madam Guyon wrote one of the greatest classics on prayer called 'Experiencing the depths of Jesus Christ'. It has enriched the prayer lives of countless millions of Christians down the years. She wrote:

> "Dear child of God, all your concepts of what God is really like amount to nothing. Do not try to imagine what God is like. Instead, simply believe in His presence. Never try to imagine what God will do. There is no way God will ever fit into your concepts. What then shall you do? Seek to behold Jesus Christ by looking to Him in your inmost being, in your spirit."

Father Jim Borst (MHM) in 'A Method of Contemplative Prayer' (Asian Trading Corporation. Bombay. 1992) observes that there are three kinds of Christian prayer. First there is vocal prayer, using a set liturgy or spontaneous words; second there is meditative prayer, centred in a mind which seeks understanding and which thinks of God; finally, there is contemplative prayer...a prayer of the heart which reaches out to God's presence. He concludes that...

> "Contemplative prayer is the only real prayer, in the sense that it leads beyond words and thoughts to the reality towards which words and thought point. In this sense, all prayer must have a contemplative quality. Now the reality we seek is spiritual reality, a reality of our own spirit, but pre-eminently the reality of the Spirit of God."

One of my hopes and dreams for the Christians of the coming generation is that that they will take seriously the need for a focussed life of prayer. Their lives must model that prayer leads us to a richer quality of life, a more healthy perspective, and a holistic perception of ourselves.

Our aim should be to reach that quality of prayer which the fourteenth century mystic Dame Julian of Norwich described in 'Revelations of Divine Love.' (The English Mystics of the Fourteenth Century. Translated by Karen Armstrong.1991. Kyle Cathie Ltd).

> "When our Lord gives us the grace of revealing himself to our soul, we have what we desire. At that time we

> are not interested in praying for anything else, because all our attention is fixed on contemplating him. This is a very exalted type of prayer that cannot, in my opinion, be described, because the origin of our prayer has been united to the sight and the vision of the One to whom we pray; wondering, enjoying, venerating, fearing him with such sweetness and delight that for the duration we can only pray in the way that he inspires us. "

Committed Christians must demonstrate that our inner life is as important to us as the creeds we recite or the doctrines we squabble about.

In the future there will be little interest in the cerebral theological analysis of our believing. The question on every-one's lips will be far more pragmatic.... for they will ask... 'does it work for you?' and 'could it work for me?'

Conclusion

John Wesley's theology respected the authority of the Bible. He opposed the domination of reason which his Anglican contemporaries so appreciated, and he defied the reliance on 'feelings' which was strongly advocated by revivalists. Wesley chose a middle way, an awesome respect for the Bible, but interpreted in the light of reason, church tradition and personal experience.

His evangelistic fervour and his advocacy of 'the strangely warmed heart' challenged the cold deism of the established church; but he fiercely protected his followers from the fanaticism which England had seen in the previous century.

Emerging church leaders must guard the flock, lest feelings become more paramount than the Bible.

Whilst the society of the new millennium may hunger for a 'spiritual feeling', it must be a spirituality based on the unchanging and eternal facts of the Gospel of Jesus Christ.

Evangelistic, Transformational Communities

Rev Steve Wild

Steve Wild is Director of Evangelism at Cliff College with a national role for resourcing local church mission. Previously he was District Evangelism Enabler in Cornwall, building up a large multi-church evangelism team. He is a much loved speaker and preacher.

Introduction

Communities are important to God. Our earliest insight into the Christian community is given to us by Luke, in the last few verses of chapter 2 of the Acts of the Apostles. He is describing an evangelistic, transformational community, which met daily, attending the temple and breaking bread together in their homes. 'And the Lord added to their number day by day those who were being saved.'[1] David Bosch points out that, like the other evangelists, Matthew wrote his gospel not as a biography of Jesus, but to 'provide guidance to a community in crisis about how it should understand its calling and mission.'[2] So, from the beginning, our mission - the way we should function to transform others as we have been transformed - has been the main item on the Church's agenda. It is in Matthew that we first find the use of the Greek word, '*ecclesia*' (called out) for the church and it is helpful to realise that all through the centuries of Christian witness the forming of communities gathered around the word and the sacraments and sending believers into the world is our mission.

I no longer have a particular local congregation to minister to; I travel around the country and 'tap in' to Christian groups who welcome me. On reflection I always find it deeply moving that, for those few hours I have been, as the Cornish put it '*one of we*', part

1 Acts ch 2 v 47
2 Bosch D, Transforming Mission (Orbis: New York 1999 p 57)

of 'the church', absorbed into them, connected, sharing because of the same Holy Spirit in them and me .... it's special.

One of my heroes is Dr Lesslie Newbigin who wrote profoundly the year before I was born about Christian community:

> 'It is surely a fact of inexhaustible significance, that what our Lord left behind Him was not a book, nor a creed, not a system nor a thought, nor a rule of life but a visible community. He committed the entire work of Salvation to that community. It was not that a community gathered around an idea, so that the idea was primary and the community secondary, the actual community is primary - the understanding of what it is comes second." [3]

So how do we turn the communities to whom we minister into evangelistic, transformational communities?

Our Wesleyan heritage has a strong line on transformational communities which they called 'societies.' They had scores of rules and regulations to keep them focused and asked once every three months, 'What is the state of the work of God amongst us?'[4] They sang, 'He bids us build each other up; and, gathered into one, to our high calling's glorious hope we hand in hand go on.'[5] This may be seen as idealistic but it is good to have a high ideal and to want the best.

Love

The key to our high ideal is shown in Paul's letter to the Romans when he writes, '*God demonstrates his own love for us in that while we were still sinners Christ died for us.*'[6] Like everybody else I can feel 'unlovely' and get weighed down in my mistakes and guilt, yet this amazing, incredible love is for unlovely me! 'Amazing love! How can it be that thou, my God, should'st die for me?'[7] That is the

3 Newbigin L. 'The Household of God' (SCM: London 1953) p82
4 Williams H. 'The Constitution and Polity of Wesleyan Methodism (Wesleyan Book Room: London 1880) p88
5 Hymns and Psalms 753 v 2
6 Romans ch 5 v 8
7 Hymns and Psalms 216 v 1

limitless length, strength and power of God's love for us. John and Charles Wesley were inspired by this love and that spread the fire of revival throughout England.

Any local Church community with an effective evangelistic urge has, at its centre, deep love for Jesus and each other. There is an attractive loveliness about this and the leader needs above all other skills the love for the people whom he/her serves – it is so easy to be critical and cynical. But my experience is that kneeling with your folk at the foot of the cross, bathed in that tender love which the Spirit brings, being fully aware of their imperfections and wrong agendas and all of them aware that you their leader also has imperfections and faults, is the launching pad for becoming an evangelistic transformational church. It is a risky endeavour and you are liable to be hurt because you are vulnerable. The great encouragement is that you do not do it alone – the foot of the cross may be a place sometimes for personal solitude but you are never alone there.

Prayer

Flowing from the love that the Spirit brings comes prayer. Some people are very shy around prayer. They will talk about almost anything else but their prayer journey – this can sometimes be because their prayer is non-existent, but not always. I've known fellowships, large and small with amazing premises, good funds, well run organisations and groups, but the prayer life is like the 'King's New Clothes' in the Hans Christian Andersen story; they're spiritually naked – yet everyone is saying how marvellous it all is!

My findings may sound very basic and un-dynamic, but I've counted getting individuals and church fellowships to take God seriously in prayer, among my major triumphs.

This again involves vulnerability. Years ago Rob Frost did a prayer tour called 'Pilgrims'. I took folk from my Circuit to join in and my jaw hit the floor as Rob, an evangelist I've admired since I first met him when he was a theological student, spoke of the struggles he had in his prayer life. To hear Rob say he didn't find prayer easy made the pedestal I'd put him on wobble. Yet, as I thought more about it, I began to understand something deeper about the journey of prayer and that, although for some gifted people prayer may be easy, most of us struggle and have to find a structure to help discipline ourselves. The Principal of Cliff College in the 1920's and 30s, Samuel Chadwick, whose prayer life is legendary, wrote: 'the practice of private prayer is so difficult to maintain.....'[8] But a regular sustained prayer life is possible and very fulfilling, whilst helping others and seeing them develop as praying people is equally exciting.

I've found that offering more than one way of praying, being open to different styles of prayer, helps a congregation to get more tuned in to the spiritual energy available. I remember two couples who had been brought up in the same area; attended the same chapel since marriage over 30 years before but who had never prayed together or really talked about prayer. They insisted that praying 'out loud' was not their style so in the end they began a fortnightly session where they would have an evening meal together and then sit in the front room with a piece of Christian music playing for a side of the tape and in silence they would pray. Fine, I'm always happy that people pray in their way and particularly as they said that it was helpful, but things developed over time. First, one side of the tape was not long enough and then they started to light a candle on the coffee table. When a woman in the church was seriously ill everyone focused their prayers on her, and they told me how when focusing on her at their prayer time one of the blokes burst out with, 'O God please heal Angie!' Since then occasionally prayers are verbalised, and their prayer life is growing. People can learn to pray and when they do things start to happen.

Focus

The title of the popular book 'The Purpose Driven Church'[9] helps us to see what it means to have a clear focus. The 'Purpose (ie Mission) Statement' of the Saddleback Church, California is, *'To bring people to Jesus and membership in his family, develop them to Christ-like maturity and equip them for their ministry in the*

8 Chadwick S 'The Path of Prayer' (Cliff College: Sheffield 1991) p 27

9 Warren R ' The Purpose Driven Church' (Zondervan: Grand Rapids 1995)

church and life mission in the world, in order to magnify God's name.'

Any local Christian congregation which seeks to be an evangel-istic transformational community needs a clear aim. We may yawn at mission statements and think they are just another piece of bureaucracy but I find churches that have carefully thought through their mission statement and used it to head the notice sheet, church note-paper, even the outside notice board, have benefited greatly.

It must be said in all honesty that, because we are all fallible human beings, we will never fully get everyone on board. Accept that, and keep on loving the dubious, whilst watching that those who oppose change don't get into a place of too much power to obstruct the agreed vision. They may leave and go down the road to the local URC or Baptist; bless them, may they be happy there. But see to it that the local leadership is clear in its purpose and the people are in unity and harmony, and understand how important that is. Always be clear in communicating with one another, the devil loves it when we are hazy and think the other person knows. Let 'belt and braces'[10] be your watchword!

Working together

Trusting and using others in the task is very important. The founder of the Salvation Army, General William Booth, is recorded as saying to one of his finest evangelists, 'Never forget that it is not what you do yourself as much as what you get others to do that will be the making of the army.'[11] I've seen it so many times over the years: a fine evangelistic ministry held back by the gifted minister not allowing other people to take a lead. On a number of occasions I've asked such people why they don't allow the other talented people in the church to do things, and they have all more or less said the same thing, 'They just can't do it as well as it should be done, it's often quicker for me to do it myself'. I've responded 'You are

10 This is a colloquial phrase from Lancashire it means: 'to stop your trousers falling down wear belt and braces.'

11 Hattersley R 'Blood and Fire' (Little Brown: London 1999) p248

probably right – but if you get someone else to do it they are doing it. Maybe not as well, but if they do it, you are free to do something else and they have learned a skill - you will have empowered them.'

To enable a church to become a fully evangelistic, transform-ational community there must be a well organised team. This group are not to be the leader's clones but rather a mixed group with a fund of goodwill, united in purpose and with clear boundaries. Michael Green, writing of his amazing fruitful ministry, reflects on his time in Oxford and describes how effectively that church worked with teams.[12] Although he is speaking of a large number of young students the principle can work with a much wider age range. In one Circuit where I served, two lady Local Preachers each nursed and loved a small rural chapel until the chapels closed. The Lord used them in wonderful ways and they gave a level of pastoral care which I as the minister could never have given, and the closures involved no bad blood or arguments. In fact we did all we could to evangelise and reach out but the elderly folk surrendered! I had provided a weekly breakfast and Bible study to support them and prayed for them and with them – but they freed me to do other effective work which they couldn't have done.

Individuals

An evangelistic transformational community needs to focus on the 'one'. No matter how large a group the community is seek to aim for one person to win for Christ. One is achievable, and the each one matters. Jesus' concern for the 'ones' is shown in the gospel records. The 'sheep and goats' parable is about Jesus noticing the individual: 'as you did it to one of the least of these you did it to me'[13]; as is the miracle healing of the man born blind: ' As he passed by, he saw...'[14]. Also, in the trio of wonderful 'lost and found' parables of Luke ch 15, Jesus had noticed the one lost sheep, coin and son.

---

12 Green M. 'Adventure of Faith' (Zondervan: Grand Rapids 2001) p188

13 Matthew ch 25 v 31 - 46

14 John ch 9 v 1

To get a church to hope and pray for 'one' can be an energising experience as they see answers to their prayers, often in unexpected ways.

Of course sometimes a community can be let down. Sin and ego get the better of even the most godly and a community can be shattered. This needs to be dealt with spiritually by the leadership and then the group moves forward to a healing place. It is incredible how the Holy Spirit can use these difficult times. The late Brother Roger of Taize often talked of 'mercy'. He said,

> 'The spirit of mercy disposes the heart of stone to become a heart of flesh. It leads to a strong love.... love your neighbour as yourself. We need a great deal of goodwill towards ourselves to realize God's kindness and love for us and, in our turn, to lavish kindness upon others.'[15]

Grace and healing can be a mighty testimony in a transforming community.

Invitation

Teach people to become an inviting community. I once went to the 'ballet', not my usual haunt. A non-church-attending neighbour had met me on the road and after polite conversation asked me if I'd like to attend a forthcoming production by the local company. Their grand-daughter was one of the cast and they were so proud. Ballet isn't my cup of tea but, because he and his wife were such kind helpful people, I promised I would go. I felt apprehensive but needn't have – it was a good experience. I wouldn't go back next week but I can't say I didn't enjoy it. Mind you, he didn't tell me that the ticket cost seven pounds!

I hate to be a statistic but my reaction proves a recently produced figure that if we are invited to attend an event by someone who is a friend or someone whom we trust, a large percentage of us will agree go to with them. We might only go once but we will go.

When I look back on my years as a Circuit Minister I remember members of my congregation bringing relatives to a service at the

15 Brico R. Taize, Brother Roger and his Community (Collins: London.1978) p155

church. These people attended church in their hometown. But I can hardly remember a well-established Church Member bringing someone new to one of our services.

Why is this? Could it be that we are embarrassed or that taking a new friend will inevitably mean less time with established church friends - certainly the invitation means an adjustment to normal routine. At one church I visited the minister had done good work with a funeral follow-up and the widow said she would like to worship at the church. A staunch reliable couple lived near the widow and he asked them if they could pick her up on their way to church. It seems so easy but the whole Sunday routine of this couple was messed up. The lady wasn't always ready when they called and they had to wait, thus being late for hymn-book duty; at the close of the service the widow didn't want to stay for coffee as she felt awkward and didn't know anyone. The lady of the couple always loved the coffee time and chat with her friends. This caused tension between the couple and the widow.

That church couple would no doubt be amongst the 'hand wringing' people at the circuit meeting who bemoan the steady decline of membership, yet they could not make adjustments to their Sunday schedule to bring in one new person to their local church. I don't particularly like the phrase 'comfort zone' but many Methodists are in one; going out onto the 'highways and byways' upsets the normal routine and we don't like change.

Inviting someone to church is hardly a 'Gospel Crusade', it doesn't need a budget yet it is effective if we have the courage to ask and are prepared to make adjustments.

Years ago as a Cliff College Evangelist I conducted a frustrating mission at a Church where every evening before the 'rally' we held a prayer meeting. We spent three quarters of an hour crying out to God for the 'sinners' of the area. Yet the dozen or so people at the prayer meeting had come alone or with their partner in a car. Don't get me wrong. Prayer is an essential ingredient in outreach and mission. It did appear that, paraphrasing a prayer much used in those meetings 'Lord as we are singing and preaching tonight may someone walking past the chapel be drawn inside by curiosity and hear the message and be converted' was the preferred option to actually inviting bringing and sitting with someone at that meeting.

Small group

What do we invite people to? John Wesley's genius idea was the 'Class Meeting'[16] George Hunter III points out how, in the eighteenth century, the class provided a type of family/ community during the upheaval of the industrial revolution – today's post-modern people have a hunger for community - not vague idealistic ones but tightly-knit communities of black people, gays, teenagers and so forth. Today's breakdown of the family and the mobility which removes us from human contact down our street tend to isolate people and breeds a great longing for community.

Surveys of growing churches in Britain show that all of them have an effective small group system. Alpha groups have demonstrated that the small group is a wonderful way to bring people to faith. May we go back to our roots and let this brilliant system be rediscovered. Among the new approaches to church in contemporary mission in Britain today is what has come to be known as 'Liquid Church' - meaning that like any liquid it adopts the shape of that within which it is placed. There are churches in Shoe Shops, Hospitals, Health Clubs, Barns and Caravans. The Class Meeting/community like the more recent 'Cell Church' has a lot to offer in liquid church terms. I think that, using a housegroup or class meeting in this way as a nucleus, a liquid community church could grow. As an aside it is very interesting to me that the type of liquid church I've spoken about is not a new idea; it was being practised in the late 70's/early 80's by Dr John Vincent who sold a large chapel in inner city Sheffield and bought an 'Off licence' to worship in.[17]

---

16 Hunter G. 'To Spread the Power – Church Growth in the Wesleyan Spirit' (Abingdon: Nashville 1987) p120 ff

17 Vincent J. 'Into the City' (Epworth: London 1982) p101 Although I don't agree with all his theology Dr Vincent was certainly ahead of his time with some of his innovative ideas.

Conclusion

One of my favourite John Wesley stories is of an Irish soldier who, in one of his meetings, honestly testifies '*I was going to a woman last night, when one of my comrades met and asked me if I would go to the watch-night (a service held late at night). Out of curiosity I came; but for half the sermon I minded nothing that was said, then God struck me to the heart, so that I could not stand, but dropped down to the ground. I slept alone last night..*'[18] I have no record of what became of this man but the important point is that a friend invited him and he was converted. This is evangelism: an 'Andrew' inviting his brother to meet Jesus.[19]

18 Wesley's Journal 3rd July 1750
19 John ch 1 v 42

Where are the Evangelists?

Rev Anthony Clowes

Anthony Clowes is a Methodist minister in Hoylake on the Wirral. He has worked in youth evangelism for many years and has a heart to see the releasing and mentoring of new evangelists in the local church.

In the 2002 report to the Methodist Conference *Evangelism and Evangelists in the Methodist Church,* Graham Horsley (Evangelism Policy and Church Planting Secretary) made a statement with which few Methodists at that time could disagree. He claimed that 'it has become widely recognised that making more followers of Jesus is the area of Our Calling where the Methodist Church is least confident.' Almost three years have passed since the publication of this report, and it is perhaps time to consider whether there has been any progress made in improving this situation.

From a personal perspective as an evangelical Methodist coming towards the end of pre-ordination training, I am increasingly encouraged that through such initiatives as *Our Calling,* and the more recently published *Priorities* and the growing ministry of District Evangelism Enablers across the Connexion, the profile of evangelism in our Church has begun to be raised. However, if this trend is to continue, then much work is to be done. In this chapter I will suggest that if local Methodist congregations can begin to discover and then empower the evangelists within their fellowships, the knock on effect could be a wide spread growth in confidence in evangelistic ministry.

Yet, as we begin to look more closely at the issue, it is crucial to emphasise the fact that any discussion about the specific calling and role of an evangelist must always take place with the acknowledgement of a broader framework. That is, whilst only some people will be specifically called as evangelists, the whole community is called to be evangelistic. In no sense does the ministry of an evangelist in the local church relieve others of their responsibility to fulfil the Great Commission of Christ. Put simply, whilst some are called to be *evangelists*, we are all called to *evangelise*.

Evangelists required - apply within

In recent years the issue of evangelism and evangelists has been under discussion across many of the Christian denominations. In a 2004 report written by the Church Army's Theology of Evangelism Working Party, the conclusion was that 'the ministry of the specialist evangelist is a ministry that needs to be recognised, supported and resourced by the church in our post-modern missionary context, it is a ministry that the church cannot do without.' In their book *The Shape of Things to Come,* Frost and Hirsch tell us that

> 'if we fail to make significant place for apostolic, prophetic and evangelistic type leadership in our time, it is unlikely that the emerging missional church will get footholds into the various Western contexts in which we are called to be faithful... the Western Church simply does not have enough of the apostolic, prophetic and evangelistic leadership types at present to get the job done for mission.'[1]

Whilst this statement may well reflect the current situation in the church, viewed from a more positive perspective, could it be that God has in fact already provided His church with an army of evangelists (along with prophets and apostles) who at this time are an untapped resource, sitting in our congregations? Perhaps a brief study of the calling and ministry of the evangelist from scripture will help us to answer this question.

Biblical foundations:

The word 'evangelist' in the New Testament is derived from the Greek word ευαγγελιστησ, 'a proclaimer of the gospel,' and appears in just three places. In Acts 21:8 Philip is described by

---

1 Michael Frost & Alan Hirsch, *The Shape Of Things To Come: Innovation and Mission for the 21st Century Church* (Massachusetts: Hendrickson Publishers, 2003), 180,181

Luke as 'the evangelist.' In 2 Tim 4:5 Timothy is exhorted to 'do the work of an evangelist.' Finally, in Paul's letter to the Ephesians, the office of 'evangelist' is listed along with that of apostle, prophet, pastor and teacher as a group of distinct gifts within the Christian Church:

> 'The gifts he gave were that some would be apostles, some prophets, some evangelists, some pastors and teachers, to equip the saints for the work of ministry, for building up the body of Christ, until all of us come to the unity of the faith and of the knowledge of the Son of God, to maturity, to the measure of the full stature of Christ.'
>
> Ephesians 4:11-13

The central theme of Paul's teaching in this passage is unity in diversity. As with his list of gifts in 1 Corinthians 12, Paul once more is concerned to stress to his readers that whilst people receive different gifts, all are given for 'the common good' of the body of the church. This is a point highlighted in John Stott's commentary when he states that 'the unity of the church, far from being boringly monotonous, is exciting in its diversity....because of the different gifts that Christ distributes for the enrichment of our common life.'[2]

The position of the evangelist is strengthened further when we understand that it is a gift given to the church by the 'ascended Christ' in order to continue the work which he himself began i.e. to 'fill all things' with God's glory (Eph 4:10), with its ultimate goal of attaining full maturity of faith. It is perhaps worth noting a significant difference between the lists of gifts in Romans and 1 Corinthians, and the list in Ephesians. Whilst in both Romans and Corinthians Paul appears to be listing gifts in the form of ministries or functions within the church, the Ephesians passage points towards gifts in the form particular people or ministers (verse 11). In his *Exegetical Commentary*, Ernest Best makes this point: 'the gifts are not gifts made to people but gifts of people, people who have a particular role within the church. It maybe assumed however that the charisma appropriate to the role which each is to play will

---

2 J.R.W. Stott, *The Message of Ephesians* (Leicester: IVP, 1979), 155

have been bestowed.'[3] Could it therefore be suggested that some people are born with specific giftedness? In which case an evangelist may well have a charismatic personality, with the natural ability to connect with others and present a convincing argument for a particular point of view, qualities which may have been evident before his/her conversion.

From the scriptural models of Philip and Timothy's evangelistic ministry we can conclude several points. Evangelists minister in a variety of situations. In Acts 8:1-8 we read that Philip preached to crowds of people in the city of Samaria, whilst later on he travelled towards Gaza, where he met and shared the Gospel personally with an Ethiopian eunuch. Philip also ministered to both non believers outside the church (Acts 8:40) and within a settled congregation (Acts 21:8). In his *New International Biblical Commentary* Arthur Patzia writes that 'in the early church there were itinerant individuals who would move about into unevangelised areas in order to proclaim the gospel. However, an evangelist may also have the gift of making the gospel understandable or of leading individuals to accept it as God's word for them.'[4] As for Timothy, whilst we have a clear picture of him as an assistant missionary, taking the gospel far and wide with Paul in the book of Acts, by the time of the writing of the second pastoral and Paul's exhortation to Timothy to 'do the work of an evangelist' (2 Tim 4:5), Paul is a prisoner in Rome and Timothy is pastoring a settled congregation in Ephesus.

Therefore, by examining the relevant New Testament texts we can establish that evangelists (along with apostles, prophets, pastors and teachers) are the ascended Christ's gifts to his church, and it could be argued that these gifts are given in the form of individuals who have a natural ability in a given area. Secondly, evangelists work within the unity of the church, with the purpose of building up of the body of fellowship. Finally, evangelists operate in a number of different ways. They may minister to large groups of people, or to individuals on a more intimate basis. Whilst traditionally evangelists

---

3 E. Best, *A Critical and Exegetical Commentary on Ephesians* (Edinburgh: T & T Clark, 1998), 388

4 A.G. Patzia, *New International Biblical Commentary, Ephesians, Colossians, Philemon* (Massachusetts: Hendrickson, 1984), 240

have been viewed as those who minister primarily to the 'unconverted' outside the church, scripture leads us to conclude that they also have a distinct role and purpose within the church. With these Biblical foundations considered, we will now consider several ways in which Methodist churches and their leaders might begin to discover and then empower the evangelists that God has placed within their congregations. These will include: taking risks, discerning potential, sharing faith stories and changing cultures.

Taking risks

In recent times various church reports have attempted to set out a criterion for recognising and testing someone's call to be an evangelist, with several lists having been compiled in order to identify the desired attributes. Such lists have included:

- active membership of the local church
- a personal experience of Jesus
- a regular spiritual discipline and study of the scriptures
- a mature understanding of the Gospel and an enthusiasm for passing on the good news to others
- some understanding of the way in which the gospel relates to their own context at work and at home and the ethical issues that arise
- some understanding of the breadth of evangelism approaches and methods

Whilst there can be no doubt that looking for such qualities in those individuals with evangelistic potential is important, particularly for the individual's long term development, could it be argued that the use of such a 'tick list' for discerning an evangelist is a little too 'safe.' Indeed, I would suggest that anyone who is able to confidently tick all of the above would most probably be a mature Christian. Where, therefore, does this leave the new Christian, who in their bubbling enthusiasm just can't stop talking about Jesus, or the teenage evangelist who can't relate to traditional church, yet desperately wants their friends to discover God in the way that they have, or the individual with a simple faith who struggles to comprehend the latest evangelism strategy?

My concern is that if the church waits until an individual shows appropriate levels of maturity and understanding before recognising and affirming them as evangelists then we are in danger of 'missing the boat.' Indeed, I contend that if we want to begin to unlock and release a desperately needed army of evangelists within our churches, now is the time to 'take risks' with our people by setting them free and encouraging them to use their God-given gifts, whilst at the same time supporting and mentoring them as they begin to fulfil their potential.

When I think back to the early stages of my own Christian life (I became a Christian aged 17 through a Methodist Youth Fellowship), I am enormously grateful to those individuals who were prepared to take risks with me by giving me opportunities to learn and grow. A few weeks after my conversion experience, my Minister asked me if I'd join him in leading a local high school assembly, which I agreed to do. Since my own school experience had not been positive (I had left as soon as I was able to) I recall how nervous I felt as we drove out of our village to a local town on the morning of the assembly. As we stood at the front of the school hall ready to begin, I watched the students file in from the back, hundreds of them, not much younger than I was. After a brief introduction I was asked if I would tell the students about my faith story and something about a mission that I was hoping to be involved in. To this day I can remember very little of what I said. I think that I spoke for about five minutes, after which we sang one of those dull school assembly hymns. However, what I do remember as if it were yesterday, was the young lady with a beaming smile who approached us as we were leaving the building. She was desperate to share how fantastic she thought it was that we had talked about Jesus in her assembly. As we drove away from the school I was exhilarated. This was the first time that I'd shared my testimony, and it felt so good.

I tell this story to illustrate the point that my own passion for evangelism began with my Minister risking his own credibility by taking me into that school and allowing me to speak. Indeed, this was the first of many such 'learn and grow' opportunities that my local church leaders provided for me as a new Christian, all of which took place within a secure framework of advice, encouragement and when necessary, correction. During the seventeen years since that assembly I have had the privilege of developing an evangelistic ministry, and have worked as a full time Youth Evangelist for eight years. I feel sure that the first spark of my calling happened here.

Perhaps the ultimate example of risk taking can be found in Luke chapter 9 as we read the account of Jesus sending out the twelve. Until now, the role of the disciples had largely been one of observing Jesus' ministry, but things were about to change. When reading this passage it is important to remember that the revelation of who Jesus actually is had not yet been fully understood by the twelve, indeed Peter's Confession followed later. In his commentary on Luke, Leon Morris tells us that 'there were signs that His ministry in Galilee would not last much longer and it was important both to spread the message of the Kingdom and to give the disciples experience.'[5] I wonder what the disciples talked about as they set off on this, their first mission to 'preach the Kingdom of God'? They were hardly expert missionaries at this stage. Indeed, I doubt whether any of these 'amateur evangelists' would make the grade on an evangelist's job application today! Nigel McCulloch (Chair of the Decade of Evangelism Steering group) remarks that the disciples 'never knew what to expect especially when he sent them out relatively untrained. The twelve learned how to evangelise by doing it.'[6]

However, by the time of their second missionary experience (Luke 9), we can read of the excitement of Jesus' followers who returned 'in great joy' describing all that they had seen and done in Jesus' name. McCulloch states that 'Jesus took the risk of sending his disciples out and God is ready to do the same now in sending out the disciples of this generation.'[7] This is surely a principle that the church needs to take seriously.

---

5 Leon Morris, *Luke: Tyndale New Testament Commentaries* (London: Inter Varsity Press, 1974), 162

6 Nigel McCulloch, *A Gospel To Proclaim* (London: Darton, Longman and Todd, 1992), 26

7 Nigel McCulloch, *A Gospel To Proclaim*, 26

Discerning potential

In his book *Courageous Leadership* Bill Hybels (senior Pastor at Willow Creek) states that a key aspect in the process of discovering the gifts that God has given to us is those individuals who spot our potential at an early stage and then set about creating opportunities for these gifts to be used and developed. Hybels argues that those in leadership have a particularly important role in this process, stating that 'a discerning pastor will recognise an individual's passion and motivation and encourage that person to enter into new areas of ministry.' Speaking about his own father he writes how 'to build on my potential he intentionally threw me into all kinds of challenging, high-risk situations, even at a very early age.'[8] In a recent questionnaire I asked twelve individuals who are currently working in the area of evangelism (11 Methodist District Evangelism Enablers and 1 Director of Evangelism), what had been the significant factors in helping them to discover and develop their gifts in evangelism. Eight of the twelve stated that for them a major factor had been the encouragement of one or more significant individuals. The people included in this role of encourager ranged from former Superintendent Ministers to childhood Sunday School Teachers and close friends who had been prepared to journey alongside them. God has given gifts to his church.

Therefore, perhaps one of the most important roles of a church leader is helping the individuals in our congregations to discover what their particular gifts are and how and where they can begin to minister. As I have stated previously, this process does involve risk. As leaders part of our calling is to walk alongside God's people, setting an example for them to follow and encouraging them to learn from their successes and mistakes, in order that their gifts might develop and flourish.

Sharing faith stories

The thing that I miss most about my Cliff College student days is hearing people testify about what God was doing in their lives. During our weekly pattern of home groups and worship services students were encouraged to share both the joys and pains of their

8 Bill Hybels, *Courageous Leadership* (Michigan: Zondervan, 2002), 124

walk with God. During the mission programme testimonies were a regular feature of school assemblies, youth events and Sunday Services. I must have heard more than a hundred testimonies during my two years at Cliff, yet no two were ever the same and all of them served to encourage me personally to keep going with God.

Therefore, when McCulloch writes that 'the natural unselfconscious testimony of the ordinary Christian is worth countless sermons in the church,'[9] I suggest that he is making a crucial point. Unfortunately, most Methodist churches today appear to have forgotten the enormous value of testimony in their fellowships, despite the rich tradition of such that is clearly evident in the formation of our church. In his book 'Methodist Spirituality,' Gordon Wakefield tells us that the early Methodist societies were based on the injunction of the letter of James: 'Confess your faults to one another and pray for one another that ye may be healed.'[10] At the weekly meetings each member of a class was encouraged to share 'the state of their souls,' thus developing a sense of accountability. Counsel was given (primarily from the appointed Class Leader), and any grievances amongst members were resolved, all in an atmosphere of praise and prayer. Along with the confession of sin, testimony was shared of the power of God to help to overcome temptations and difficulties. I wonder what impact a rediscovery of this mutual accountability and faith sharing would have in our modern movement?

Changing cultures

During my time as a Youth Evangelist in Liverpool, my colleagues and I attempted to develop a variety of programmes where young people could learn to share their faith stories. The most effective of these were Cell Groups, mission trips and a form of Mission Band which we called the 'Youth Worship Team' (YWT). As young people became Christians and started to move on with God they were encouraged to share their experiences in their small groups, and occasionally at the YWT-led services in local churches. The impact

9 Nigel McCulloch, *A Gospel To Proclaim*, 30

10 Gordon Wakefield, *Exploring Methodism: Methodist Spirituality* (Peterborough: Epworth Press, 1999), 12

that this had upon the youth ministry programme and the wider church life soon became apparent. In an atmosphere where talking openly about your faith was the norm, even the shyest of individuals felt able to share. During the YWT-led services congregations were inspired as they listened to young people talking about living for God. Good news travels fast, and soon the YWT were being invited to take services far and wide. Apart from the obvious benefits for both speaker and hearer, when testimonies were shared we soon began to notice something else; even in the very early stages of their faith some members of the group quickly began to demonstrate the gifts of an evangelist. Indeed, when these young people spoke about their faith, the power and presence of God was almost tangible.

In his Grove Book *The Work and Office of an Evangelist,* David Sanderson's analysis of a survey of fifty practising evangelists reveals some interesting findings. He discovered that '60% (30) said they were involved in organised evangelistic activity at the time of their call and over 50% (27) said that their evangelistic gift was recognised by others.'[11] This is a pattern reflected in my own Christian life. It was during a two week mission with the 'Teen Challenge' organisation just six months into my faith journey that I first began to acknowledge that evangelism (a word which meant little to me at that time) was to be my life long calling. What a privilege it is to be a part of a mission team and watch those around us blossom as they begin to use their God given talents.

McCulloch concludes that 'the surest way to strengthen the faithful is to entrust them with an immediate missionary task, so that the training and the exercise go hand in hand.'[12] It is my firm conviction that when we are prepared to take risks with people and help facilitate opportunities for faith sharing (whether they be new believers or life long members), we will begin to discover those individuals whom God has set apart to be evangelists.

---

11 David Sanderson, *The Work and Office of an Evangelist: Grove Evangelism Series 31* (Nottingham: Grove Books Limited, 1995), 21

12 Nigel McCulloch, *A Gospel To Proclaim*, 26

Questions for further reflection:

- What gifts has God given you to use in His church?
- Who are the evangelists in your church?
- What opportunities are there for sharing testimony and faith sharing in the life of your church?
- How are the members of your church encouraged to discover and use their ministry gifts?

Implications for the local church

As I have stated previously, it is my view that the discovery and empowerment of evangelists in local Methodist congregations will assist in the process of renewing a sense of confidence in sharing the Good News of Jesus. As we recognise and release passionate evangelists to minister and model good practice in our local congregations others will be encouraged to join them, and the body of Christ will be built up. Evangelists come in all shapes and sizes. Whilst some will be comfortable in a leadership role speaking to large congregations, others will be more at ease 'gossiping the Gospel' in a more intimate setting. As suggested earlier, there is a clear biblical mandate for this variety of interpretation and as such both should be recognised and encouraged.

The ministry of an evangelist is often by its very nature groundbreaking. In his book *The Evangelist's Notebook,* John Peters uses the term 'adventurer' when attempting to describe the evangelist's personality type. Peters suggests that 'adven-turers are innovators, easily bored, needing wide open spaces, enormous challenge and substantially untrammelled freedom if they are to flourish,'[13] I therefore contend that an inevitable result of discovering and empowering the evangelists in our congregations will be a renewed desire to push the boundaries of the church. As new, outward focused ministries are launched, previously untapped areas of the community could be reached with the gospel message. John Stott argues that 'there is a great need for gifted evangelists today who will pioneer new ways of exercising and developing their

13 John Peters, *Ministry Guides – The Evangelists Notebook* (Eastbourne: Kingsway Publications, 2002), 64

gift, so as to penetrate the vast unreached segments of society for Christ.'[14]

I wonder however, what forms of church might begin to emerge if our 'adventurers' were released to pioneer new forms of ministry? If indeed they were touched by the Gospel of Christ, how would these 'vast unreached segments of society' relate to and express their new found faith within our traditional forms of church? I suggest that for many of them the cultural gap would be a leap too far. Therefore, perhaps our challenge is to encourage and support our adventurers as new expressions of church (which may be foreign to our own experience and not necessarily our personal preference) begin to take shape around them.

Unfortunately such encouragement and support has not been the experience for some evangelists, particularly those in the traditional denominations, and some have become frustrated and misunderstood. When an individual's primary focus for their Christian service is reaching the lost by any means possible, it is perhaps inevitable that some evangelists have become disillusioned when their churches appear to be more inward than outward looking. Graham Horsley expresses this concern when he writes that 'evangelists finding little opportunity for employment within the denominational structures have often gone to para-church agencies or become freelance entrepreneurs.'[15] Frost and Hirsch make similar claims when they suggest that 'some evangelists are forced to express their innate gifting in contexts other than the established local church or denomination.'[16]

Clearly, this should be a cause for great concern to the modern Methodist Church. If British Methodism is to stem the current trend of decline then it is crucial that we hold tight to the evangelists that God has given to us, give them a voice to be heard in the wider

---

14 J.R.W. Stott, *The Message of Ephesians*, 163

15 Graham Horsley, 'The Role and Recognition of Evangelists' in *Over To You: Reports from the Methodist Conference 2000* (Peterborough: Methodist Publishing House, 2000),100-112,105

16 Michael Frost & Alan Hirsch, *The Shape Of Things To Come: Innovation and Mission for the 21ST Century Church*, 179

church and journey alongside them as they offer themselves in God's service.

Finally, and perhaps most importantly of all, as we recognise and release the evangelists in our congregations it is vital that all of God's people stand alongside them in prayer. Evangelists, by very nature will find themselves on the frontline of the church's missionary activity. Without continued prayer support these individuals will be vulnerable to disillusionment and spiritual attack. As Paul writes, 'for our struggle is not against flesh and blood, but against the rulers, against the authorities, against the powers of this dark world and against the spiritual forces of evil in the heavenly realms.' (Eph 6:12).

Questions for further reflection:

- How do you affirm those with evangelistic gifting in your church?
- What are the possibilities for new expressions of church in your community?
- How often do you pray for your 'frontline' evangelists?

Conclusion
William Porter

'Effective leaders concentrate on the things they are able to change; ineffective leaders spend their energy on things they are very unlikely ever to be able to change.' Anon

The world is changing fast. God wants His church to creatively engage in responding to that change. We are privileged to be part of a generation in which our influence is significant towards the shaping of 21st century Christianity. God desires to use us as change agents to affect a church and a world for Christ. Leadership is crucial, but we can only offer to God what previous generations of leaders have done – ordinary, weak, fallible human beings whom He might use to make a kingdom difference.

God's heart, I believe, is to impart His missionary DNA into His church. What does that look like? It looks like many things but, at its cutting edge, it looks like the priorities of ministry we have set out. These cutting edge themes of ministry are not the sum total of the gospel; they aren't the fully orbed ministry of the church. Yet these four areas are crucial if we have our eyes fixed on Jesus, and are willing to follow the guidance of His Spirit: mobilising a movement of prayer that helps us again become God centred; sparking spiritual renewal, as we seek holiness, anointing and freshness of Spirit life; releasing radical leaders, in a servant-empowering way, even at a cost to ourselves; enabling churches to become evangelistic communities again, transformational in impact. If we do these things, I believe that God can intentionally position us for waves of revival and times of harvest amongst the lost that we long for in our generation.

My hope is that this resonates where many leaders of God's church are at. God is calling for a generational change – a sea change in church, where we are moving out in increasing waves of Spirit anointed, authentic, mission-focused expressions of church over a generation to turn our nation round. It is what happened in Wesley's day, it is what happened with the Clapham Sect, it is what happened in South American Pentecostalism, it is what is happening in latter 20th century China, it is what is happening at the start of this century in parts of the African continent. Revival brings a generational sea change.

To return to the harvest image in my introduction: at the front of the book is a picture by American artist Tom Hammond. It is a vignette of old time revival. The church in the middle of the corn field is hit by a lightning strike on the spire, and the sign outside reads 'revival in progress'. I believe it is a parable of our churches right now. The church might look outdated, but we're asking God for a lightning strike of His Spirit again, to infuse us with His missionary DNA, and to send us out into the harvest.

We are in the vanguard of making this possible. The course we define will be the one our children will follow; the path we lead them on will be one of life-renewing or death-defining. May God help us play our part faithfully, and run our race well.